KEEPING GOOD TEACHERS

Edited by
MARGE SCHERER

 ASSOCIATION FOR SUPERVISION AND CURRICULUM DEVELOPMENT ~ ALEXANDRIA, VIRGINIA ~ USA

Association for Supervision and Curriculum Development
1703 N. Beauregard St. • Alexandria, VA 22311-1714 USA
Telephone: 800-933-2723 or 703-578-9600 • Fax: 703-575-5400
Web site: http://www.ascd.org • E-mail: member@ascd.org

Gene R. Carter, *Executive Director;* Nancy Modrak, *Director of Publishing;* Julie Houtz, *Director of Book Editing & Production;* Ernesto Yermoli, *Project Manager;* Deborah Perkins-Gough, *Senior Associate Editor;* Sally Lindfors, *Associate Editor;* Miriam Goldstein, *Associate Editor;* Kevin Davis, *Project Assistant;* Georgia McDonald, *Senior Graphic Designer;* Keith Demmons, *Typesetter;* Tracey A. Smith, *Production Manager.*

Printed in the United States of America.

s12/03

Paperback ISBN: 0-87120-862-8 • ASCD product #104138 • List Price: $28.95 ($22.95 ASCD member price, direct from ASCD only)

e-books ($28.95): netlibrary ISBN 0-87120-953-5 • ebrary ISBN 0-87120-943-8

Library of Congress Cataloging-in-Publication Data

Keeping good teachers / edited by Marge Scherer.
     p. cm.
Includes bibliographical references and index.
  ISBN 0-87120-862-8 (alk. paper)
  1. Teachers--Training of--United States. 2. Teachers--In-service training--United States. 3. Mentoring in education--United States. I. Scherer, Marge, 1945- II. Association for Supervision and Curriculum Development.

  LB1715.K34 2003
  370'.71'5--dc22

                                        2003020715

13 12 11 10 09 08 07 06 05 04 03   12 11 10 9 8 7 6 5 4 3 2 1

KEEPING GOOD TEACHERS

Introduction

Achieving Staying Power

Marge Scherer

Seven years ago when Mel Riddile became principal of J.E.B. Stuart High School in Fairfax County, Virginia, there was—as is not uncommon when new principals take charge of a school—significant teacher turnover. Contributing to the situation, recent retirement system changes were creating a mass exodus of experienced teachers throughout the state. In total, 22 percent of the 130 teaching positions at Stuart were open that year—the equivalent of 28 and one-half full-time spots.

The teacher turnover rate was only one of the challenges that the school faced. Back in 1996, Stuart was the lowest performing high school of 24 in the county and had the worst student attendance rate. It was then, and still is, number one in the county in three risk factors that predict low student achievement: student poverty (54 percent of the students qualify for free or reduced lunch); mobility (family mobility is 30 percent); and a primary language other than English. Of the 1,500 students enrolled, 30 percent are Hispanic, 27 percent white, 20 percent Asian, 12 percent Middle Eastern, and 11 percent black. Seventy percent of Stuart students were born outside the United States, and for two-thirds of them, English is not their native language.

In 2003, Stuart's academic picture is much improved. Today the dropout rate is 2.8 percent, and 97 percent of students graduate. The attendance rate has improved from a little over 90 percent to 96 percent. More than 80 percent of students last year passed all 11 of the state's standardized exit exams, the same proportion that passed just one exam in 1998. Forty percent are enrolled in International Baccalaureate classes. Ninety-nine percent of the class of 2002 is attending two- or four-year colleges. And the school boasts one of the lowest teacher absenteeism rates in the school system.

What's more, Stuart will be hiring only 14 new teachers for the coming school year—about 11 percent of its teaching staff. Now when teachers leave Stuart, they still say they are lured by lower housing costs in suburbs farther from Washington, D.C., or by a reduction of commuting time in a traffic-choked region. But today, if they mention that they have been wooed away by another school, it is not so much because the new school has much more to offer, as it is because teachers have gained something special at Stuart that has made them more attractive to other schools.

Stuart's Turnaround

What did the Stuart school community do to improve its academic picture and, not coincidentally, cut its teacher turnover rate? As in every turnaround story, the reasons for Stuart's success are intermingled. Following are some of the factors experts say are likely to influence teacher staying power.

Include teachers in decision making. In 1997, principal Riddile asked teachers what factors were holding Stuart back from improving student achievement. Teachers overwhelmingly identified low attendance and poor reading skills as the priority problems.

In the ensuing years, the school launched a massive effort to curb absenteeism. The administration monitored attendance reports more frequently and initiated an automated calling system. Teachers began mentoring students with attendance problems. Stuart went from having the worst attendance record in the system to an average one.

The school community also tackled the reading issue from multiple directions, putting into place a reading lab and a reading-across-the-curriculum program and hiring a reading coach for the content teachers. Teachers adopted a direct instruction approach for students who had not yet learned to read. For those reading below grade level, a reading-to-learn program focused on comprehension, vocabulary expansion, and fluency. When teachers complained that they did not have enough of the right kinds of books, enterprising faculty began an Internet search for free and cheap books. Every teacher became a teacher of reading.

Help teachers meet the needs of their students. Not only are faculty meetings a time for teachers to make decisions, but each meeting also has an instructional component. Teachers have participated in symposiums on teaching high school youth and on teaching reading to an immigrant population. From exploring different instructional models—such as standards-based classroom instruction—to learning about technology and how to redirect the flow of instruction, teachers receive ongoing professional development. As a result, teachers say that they feel more empowered to reach students. And fine-tuning their skills has added value to their professional resumes.

Attend to the beginners. At Stuart, mentors coach beginning teachers, and buddy teachers introduce newly hired experienced teachers to the ways of the school. Both mentors and buddy teachers receive compensation for the additional work. Beginners also attend a monthly meeting customized for them where they discuss concerns, learn new strategies, and view video clips of teaching practices.

Regardless of seniority, all teachers teach a wide range of students so that the least-experienced teachers do not always work with the lowest-achieving students and the lowest-achieving students are not always taught by the least experienced teachers. The science department chair, for example, teaches a beginning ESL science class as well as an advanced class.

Get priorities straight. Stuart operates on the premise that "given sufficient time, all students can learn." And despite a strong emphasis on achievement, teachers know that long-term gains are more important than short-term gains. Small class size, double-block algebra, structured English and social studies classes, and a biology concepts class offer mastery learning opportunities. Students know that they can move to other classes as soon as they prove competency. With so many students taking International Baccalaureate courses, students are motivated to move into advanced classes. A modified calendar with two summer sessions offers extra time to those who need it and offers flexibility to teachers as well. An extended day offers more time for instruction and the extracurricular activities that raise student morale, extend learning, and make the school a friendlier place.

Improve the school climate. With the many stresses of daily life, the administration has made a conscious effort to decrease the daily irritations that can cause job dissatisfaction. The little things range from making sure that the copiers are always working, to scheduling fewer interruptions during instructional time, to turning on the air conditioning when needed, to providing food at faculty meetings. Teachers are routinely surveyed to discover the sources of dissatisfaction or ideas for improving school life. Among the most popular programs that they suggested is the weekly newsletter profile of the Teacher of the Week. On Monday morning, the principal delivers a bagel and coffee to the teacher in front of his or her class.

Keeping Good Teachers

We have known for some time that the single most important thing we can do to help students achieve high standards is to put qualified teachers in every class. Occasionally, outside critics may think that paying attention to teacher retention is a narrow, self-interested approach. But teacher retention is not something that can be easily addressed without addressing many other facets of school life. The story of J.E.B. Stuart High School suggests that the retention of good teachers comes about when a school improves itself for the sake of its students.

Stuart's experience, along with the many examples of practices and policies described in this book, suggest possibilities to educators interested in teaching all students, improving schools and, thereby, retaining good teachers. Much is at stake. As Kati Haycock of the Education Trust recently told a group of education reporters, "If we could ensure five years in a row of above-average teachers for poor children, we could close the achievement gap."

About the Book

What attracts good teachers and keeps them in the profession? What makes schools better places for students to learn and for teachers to work? These questions are at the heart of *Keeping Good Teachers*.

Both the recent federal requirement to place a "highly qualified teacher" in every classroom and an above-average turnover rate among teachers prompted the *Educational Leadership* staff to compile a theme issue ("Keeping Good Teachers," May 2003) to explore these matters. *Keeping Good Teachers*, the book, is an offshoot of that theme issue, compiled from new articles and a few favorites previously published.

The voices in these chapters come from within the profession, and the perceptions of the problems and solutions are those of insiders. Many of the chapter authors not only relate their own experience, but also survey fellow educators to find out which practices and policies are most beneficial and most practical to implement in schools.

The book begins with a section that explores the extent of the problem and sets the context for studying it. In "Responding to the Teacher Shortage," Heather Voke researches the nature of the shortage, its probable causes, the problems that result from having a dearth of qualified teachers, and the policy changes frequently recommended. Next, David C. Berliner critiques some alternative methods suggested for enlarging the teaching force, and reminds us that retention solutions must address quality as well as quantity.

In Part II, "Welcoming Teachers," authors explore the beginnings of the problem. How are the newest teachers introduced to their profession and their first school? What elements make an induction program effective, and how long should induction last? Harvard researchers Susan Moore Johnson and Susan M. Kardos describe the professional culture that beginners prefer: one that respects the needs of novices and veterans alike. Author Harry K. Wong describes structured induction programs that provide ongoing professional development.

In Part III, "Valuing Good Teachers," authors look at the issues of compensation, performance–based pay, career paths, national certification, and other ways to reward educators and make them feel valued. For example, John Schacter reports on the Milken Family Foundation's Teacher Advancement Program, a comprehensive reform based on rewarding teachers for performance. He finds that programs that increase teacher job satisfaction can also increase student achievement in formerly low-achieving schools.

In Part IV, "Supporting Good Teachers," the authors describe how principals and administrators can sustain their teachers. What special attention supports second-career teachers, graduate teacher candidates, special education teachers, and novices?

Part V, "Reflecting on What Makes Good Teachers," looks at the needs and desires of master teachers. In an effort to discover how to keep highly qualified teachers in schools where their skills are most needed, Sonia M. Nieto asks some of the most highly gifted teachers she knows to reflect on why they stay. In their answers she finds insights about how to ignite the passion and still the disenchantment that comes from doing a difficult job. Karianne Sparks and Leslie Keiler survey former teachers about what drove them away, and Mark F. Goldberg explores what makes veterans stay—and strive for excellence.

Like its predecessor *A Better Beginning: Supporting and Mentoring New Teachers* (ASCD, 1999), *Keeping Good Teachers* is dedicated to all those who want to make their profession the best it can be, and who are creating the teaching conditions where good teachers can thrive.

Part I

Keeping Good Teachers

Responding to the Teacher Shortage

Heather Voke

Heather Voke is an adjunct lecturer at the Georgetown University Department of Philosophy, New North 215, 37th and O Streets N.W., Washington, DC 20017. She also serves as a consultant on issues related to education policy for education organizations in the Washington, D.C. area. She can be reached by phone at (202) 687-2592 and by e-mail at hmv2@georgetown.edu. A longer version of this chapter appeared in the May 2002 issue of ASCD Infobrief.

Newspaper headlines dramatically declare that U.S. public schools are facing a teacher shortage of epic proportions. States respond quickly by developing and implementing new incentive and training programs to attract more teachers to the profession. According to researchers, however, the problem is much more complex than the media would have us believe, and unless the initiatives developed to address the problem take this complexity into account, at best the problem will not be addressed, and at worst, the solutions may actually exacerbate the situation (Ingersoll, 1998; National Association of State Boards of Education [NASBE], 1998).

The Nature of the Teacher Shortage

Researchers agree that climbing student enrollment, new laws requiring smaller class size, and impending retirements mean that the United States will need to attract more teachers over the next decade; however, many now disagree with initial projections, made during the 1980s and 1990s, that the country will need as many as two million new teachers. There will continue to be a shortage, these researchers say, but recent data, which allow a more accurate assessment of trends, indicate that this shortage may not be as dramatic as earlier reports predicted (Baker & Smith, 1997; Wayne, 2000).

Researchers also dispute the conventional wisdom that the shortage exists because there are simply not enough qualified teachers to fill the number of vacant positions. If we consider only the number of qualified candidates and the number of job openings, there is an overall surplus of trained people (Darling-Hammond, 2001; NASBE, 1998).

The shortage lies in the distribution of teachers. There are not enough teachers who are both qualified and willing to teach in urban and rural schools, particularly in those serving low-income students or students of color. There is also a shortage in certain geographic regions of the country, and there are not enough qualified individuals in particular specialties, such as special education, bilingual education, and the sciences (Bradley, 1999; NASBE, 1998). Some also argue that it is not an insufficient production of qualified teacher candidates that causes staff shortage, as conventional analyses maintain, but rather the high rates of teacher turnover (Ingersoll, 2000).

Given these misunderstandings about the nature of the shortage, analysts argue that the policies and initiatives the states and districts have developed to address the problem are misguided. For example, the National Association of State Boards of Education argues that programs developed by states to simply attract more people to the profession are not likely to be effective:

> Most states do not need to recruit more candidates into teacher preparation programs. Most states do not even need to attract higher quality candidates to teaching. What states do need, however, are targeted programs that attract candidates who are willing and able to meet the needs of the schools in which they will be asked to teach. (1998, p. 13)

Others argue that initiatives that seek to address the shortage by increasing the supply of candidates are not likely to be effective if they overlook the high turnover rate. These critics believe that if these initiatives are to be effective, they must focus more on retention and less on recruitment (Ingersoll, 2001).

Why Does the Shortage Matter?

The most obvious consequence of the shortage is that states, districts, and schools must invest considerable resources to attract potential candidates to fill empty positions. In addition, the shortage has important consequences for the quality of education that students receive. According to Ingersoll, principals who face difficulties in locating sufficient numbers of qualified job candidates "most commonly do three things: hire less-qualified teachers, assign teachers trained in another field or grade level to teach in the understaffed area, and make extensive use of substitute teachers" (1997, p. 42). Consequently, students are being taught by teachers who lack the knowledge and skills necessary for quality instruction. Ingersoll's research shows that almost one-third of all high school math teachers have neither a major nor a minor in math or a related discipline. Almost one-fourth of high school English teachers have neither a major nor a minor in English or a related field. Almost half of all high school students enrolled in physical science courses are taught by teachers without at least a minor in any physical science. More than half of all high school history students are taught by teachers without either a major or a minor in history (Ingersoll, 1998). As a result, "for English, math, and history, several million students a year in each discipline are taught by teachers without a major or minor in the field" (Ingersoll, 1998, p. 774).

Research shows that students in low-wealth communities are much more likely to be taught by teachers with deficient qualifications. According to Kati Haycock, director of the Education Trust:

> While the teaching force in high-poverty and high-minority communities certainly includes some of the most dedicated and talented teachers in the country, the truth is that these teachers are vastly outnumbered by under- and, indeed, unqualified candidates. . . . Minority and poor youngsters—the very youngsters who are most dependent on their teachers for content knowledge—are systematically taught by teachers with the least content knowledge. Teachers who lack even a minor in the field they are teaching are more than three times more prevalent in low-wealth schools than in those with high wealth. (1998, p. 7)

Out-of-field teaching is problematic given the effect that teacher qualifications have on student learning. According to the National Commission on Teaching and America's Future, "studies show that teacher expertise is the most important factor in student achievement" (1996, p. 6). There is also evidence that the effects of teacher quality are long-lasting and cumulative; the effects of poor-quality instruction linger and are exacerbated over time

(Darling-Hammond & Ball, 1998; Haycock, 1998). Recent research has also shown that teaching quality has an even greater effect on the achievement of at-risk students (Haycock, 1998). This is particularly troubling, given that out-of-field teaching takes place with greatest frequency in high-poverty urban and rural schools, in schools serving predominately children of color, and with students who are already achieving at lowest levels—all populations that are already at risk of school failure (Fetler, 1997; Ingersoll, 1998; Olson & Jerald, 1998).

Retaining Quality Teachers

Researchers have compared the teaching profession to a revolving door (U.S. Department of Education, 2000). They argue that school staffing problems are caused not so much by an insufficient supply of qualified individuals, but by "too many teachers leaving teaching" (Ingersoll, 1997, p. 2). For example, a U.S. Department of Education study of students who earned college degrees in 1992–1993 found that nearly one out of five who graduated from college in that year and began teaching in the public schools by 1994–1995 had left the profession by 1996–1997 (Boser, 2000). Other studies have shown that approximately one-fourth of all beginning teachers leave the classroom within the first four years (Hare & Heap, 2001a).

Turnover is particularly pronounced in certain teaching fields, such as special education, mathematics, and science (Ingersoll, 2000). Although all types of districts report problems retaining new teachers, this problem is particularly pronounced in schools located in low-income areas (Hare & Heap, 2001b; NASBE, 1998). The turnover rate for schools located in high-poverty areas, for example, can climb as high as 50 percent (Hare & Heap, 2001a).

Even more alarming than the turnover rates themselves are data suggesting that the most intelligent and effective teachers—the teachers that policymakers are most interested in retaining—leave the profession at the highest rates. In a study conducted in the Midwest, the majority of superintendents interviewed reported that from 75 to 100 percent of the teachers leaving classrooms are "highly effective" or "effective" (Hare & Heap, 2001b). Another study found that new teachers who scored in the top quartile on their college entrance exams are nearly twice as likely to leave teaching than those with lower scores (Boser, 2000).

Teacher turnover is problematic for a number of reasons. First and most obvious, it forces states, districts, and schools to devote attention, time, and financial resources to initiatives designed to attract additional candidates to replace those who leave the profession. In addition, once schools and districts hire new teachers, they must expend "enormous energies developing [these] new teachers, who are likely to leave after only a few years and be replaced by yet another recruit in need of special resources and support" (NASBE, 1998, p. 7).

Teacher turnover can also undermine schools' efforts to implement reforms; successful school reform requires sustained and shared commitment by school staff. Staff turnover means that new teachers, unfamiliar with and uncommitted to those reforms, must somehow be brought on board.

There are direct disadvantages for student learning as well. The skills and understandings that make for quality teaching take time to acquire, and research shows that new teachers are less effective at producing student learning than more experienced teachers (Hawley, 2000). Given the high turnover rate and its negative consequences, Ingersoll argues that "teacher recruitment programs alone will not solve the staffing problems of schools if they do not also address the organizational sources of low retention" (2001, p. 501).

What reasons do teachers cite for leaving their positions? Although retirement and school staffing cutbacks cause some teachers to leave, personal and family matters and job dissatisfaction are more frequently cited as reasons. According to Ingersoll (2000, 2001), 42 percent of all departees report leaving for job dissatisfaction or the desire to pursue a better job, another career, or better career opportunities. Those who report leaving because of job dissatisfaction cite low salaries, lack of support from school administration, lack of student motivation, student discipline problems, and lack of teacher influence over decision making as factors influencing their decisions.

To some degree, the reasons that teachers cite for leaving vary according to their teaching context: Teachers in rural schools are more likely to leave due to social, geographic, cultural, and professional isolation than teachers in other contexts (Collins, 1999). Teachers in urban schools report being least satisfied by access to teaching resources and control over curriculum and pedagogy (Claycomb, 2000). Teachers in small private schools report that dissatisfaction with salaries and with their schools' administration lead them to leave (Collins, 1999).

Particularly problematic for the retention of new teachers is the lack of support that they receive from their schools. New teachers interviewed by researchers from the Project on the Next Generation of Teachers reported that they received little guidance or encouragement from their new schools. For example, although most of the teachers had been formally assigned mentors, new faculty actually had few and limited opportunities to interact with those mentors (Johnson et al., 2001). Other research has shown that only 44 percent of teachers have participated in a formal first-year mentoring program, even though there is evidence that participation in such programs can reduce attrition rates by up to two-thirds (U.S. Department of Education, 2000). Project research also showed that new teachers suffer from a lack of guidance from their colleagues on what to teach and how to teach (Kauffman, Johnson, Kardos, Liu, & Peske, 2001).

New teachers are often faced with overwhelming workloads. They are frequently assigned the most challenging students, asked to teach multiple subjects, required to teach classes for which they are not certified, and assigned responsibility for overseeing extracurricular activities (U.S. Department of Education, 2000).

The current context of standards and accountability also complicates the problem of retaining new teachers and contributes to teacher turnover. As states and the federal government develop mandates related to testing and accountability, "districts are introducing new reforms and initiatives at a frenetic pace. As a result, new teachers are struggling to learn their craft in dynamic and frequently chaotic environments" (Johnson et al., 2001, p. 8).

Despite the challenges that these new teachers face, according to the researchers from the Project on the Next Generation of Teachers, "neither the structures nor the cultures of their schools seemed to be geared toward their needs as novice teachers" (Johnson et al., 2001, p. 8).

Teachers as a group report that they are dissatisfied by insufficient autonomy and control over teaching. According to Joel Spring, a historian of education, "In recent years the satisfaction that teachers have gained from autonomous decision making and creativity has been threatened by expanding bureaucratic structures and attempts to control teacher behavior in the classroom" (1996, p. 41). For example, there is evidence that the high-stakes environment associated with the standards and accountability movement has contributed to the decisions of experienced teachers to leave the profession (Hansel, Skinner, & Rotberg, 2001; Prince, 2002).

Low salaries and lack of respect from the public also pose a challenge for teacher retention. Research shows that new teachers enter teaching primarily for its intrinsic or psychological rewards—that is, the opportunity to engage in meaningful work, the pleasure of working with children, and love of a particular subject area—rather than extrinsic rewards such as salary or public respect (Goodlad, 1984; Liu, Kardos, Kauffman, Peske, & Johnson, 2000; Lortie, 1975). However, although the extrinsic rewards may not attract people to the profession, lack of satisfaction with these rewards is frequently cited as a reason for leaving.

Researchers speculate that when receipt of intrinsic rewards is thwarted (through student discipline problems, for example, or insufficient autonomy in the classroom), teachers become less willing to tolerate the low salaries and lack of public respect (Goodlad, 1984).

Policy Recommendations

What can states and districts do to better retain teachers? Researchers and analysts have suggested the following strategies:

- Increasing salaries for all teachers and developing differentiated pay scales that reward expert teachers and those who take on specialized roles and responsibilities (Grissmer & Kirby, 1997; Johnson, 2000). Reward those willing to teach in high-need areas where teacher retention is problematic by giving them higher salaries than those teaching in areas and fields in which there is a glut of qualified teachers (NASBE, 1998).
- Creating high-quality induction programs for new teachers, requiring districts to offer these programs, and providing funding to support the programs. According to Darling-Hammond, "beginning teachers who have access to intensive mentoring by expert colleagues are much less likely to leave teaching in the early years" (2000, p. 22). She cites the example of school districts, such as those in Cincinnati, Columbus, and Toledo, Ohio, who have been able to reduce the attrition rates of new teachers by more than two-thirds by connecting new teachers with expert mentors and providing both with joint release time. Such programs not only encourage new teachers to stay in the profession, but also enable them to become competent more quickly. Darling-

Hammond (2000) also recommends developing peer review systems
that focus on improving the performance of new teachers and providing professional development opportunities that are targeted to the particular needs of individual teachers.

- Developing regulations prohibiting out-of-field teaching. Implement
practices that place experienced rather than novice teachers with the
students with greatest need, provide new teachers with additional
release time, and limit their extracurricular responsibilities (Goodwin,
1999).

- Adopting policies that include teachers in school-based decision making. Increased faculty control over school policymaking and greater
teacher autonomy in the classroom are both associated with increased
teacher commitment (Grant & Murray, 1999; Ingersoll, Alsalam,
Quinn, & Bobbitt, 1997).

- Growing your own teachers. Rural and high-poverty districts and
schools should encourage graduates and paraprofessionals already
familiar with the culture and challenges associated with those environments to become certified (Collins, 1999).

- Encouraging or requiring universities to develop teacher education programs that focus on providing potential teachers with the specific skills
and knowledge necessary to succeed in schools with high turnover rates
(NASBE, 1998). For example, require schools of education to develop
teacher education programs that focus on the challenges associated
with teaching in urban schools (Claycomb, 2000).

- Implementing policies that support reduction of class size and increasing funding for quality resources, facilities, and materials in high-
poverty schools. Teachers in such schools might be given additional
preparation time, as well as access to additional professional development that focuses on the particular challenges associated with teaching
in a high-poverty, urban environment (Claycomb, 2000; NASBE,
1998).

The Challenge

The research suggests that if policymakers and education leaders do not
understand the nature of the teacher shortage, the solutions that they develop
will be ineffective in addressing that problem and may even create new prob-

lems in their wake. If states and districts react to news about the teacher shortage by developing programs that simply attract more candidates to the profession and quickly prepare them to enter the classroom, then they risk wasting valuable resources and undermining the quality of education that children receive; all programs must be designed to produce teachers who have the skills, knowledge, and commitment necessary to teach effectively in high-need areas. Similarly, if states and districts do not address the role that high teacher turnover plays relative to the teacher shortage, and they do not develop policies and initiatives that address the causes of high turnover in schools, then they will not effectively address the problem, and they will undermine efforts to provide all students with a quality education.

References

Baker, D. P., & Smith, T. (1997). Teacher turnover and teacher quality: Refocusing the issue. *Teachers College Record, 99*(1), 29–35.

Boser, U. (2000). A picture of the teacher pipeline: Baccalaureate and beyond. *Education Week Quality Counts 2000, 19*(18), 17.

Bradley, A. (1999). States' uneven teacher supply complicates staffing of schools. *Education Week, 18*(26), 1, 10–11.

Claycomb, C. (2000). High-quality urban school teachers: What they need to enter and to remain in hard-to-staff schools. *The State Education Standard, 1*(1), 17–21.

Collins, T. (1999). *Attracting and retaining teachers in rural areas.* (ERIC Digest 99–7). Charleston, WV: ERIC Clearinghouse on Rural Education and Small Schools.

Darling-Hammond, L. (2000). *Solving the dilemmas of teacher supply, demand, and standards.* New York: National Commission on Education and America's Future.

Darling-Hammond, L. (2001). The challenge of staffing our schools. *Educational Leadership, 58*(8), 12–17.

Darling-Hammond, L., & Ball, D. L. (1998). *Teaching for high standards: What policymakers need to know and be able to do.* Philadelphia, PA: National Commission on Teaching and America's Future and the Consortium for Policy Research in Education.

Fetler, M. (1997). Staffing up and dropping out: Unintended consequences of high demand for teachers. *Education Policy Analysis Archives, 5*(16) [Electronic journal]. Available: http://olam.ed.asu.edu/epaa/v5n16.html

Goodlad, J. (1984). *A place called school.* New York: McGraw-Hill.

Goodwin, B. (1999). Improving teaching quality: Issues and policies. *McREL Policy Brief.* Aurora, CO: Mid-continent Regional Educational Laboratory.

Grant, G., & Murray, C. E. (1999). *Teaching in America: The slow revolution.* Cambridge, MA: Harvard University Press.

Grissmer, D., & Kirby, S. N. (1997). Teacher turnover and teacher quality. *Teachers College Record, 99*(1), 44–57.

Hansel, L., Skinner, B., & Rotberg, I. C. (2001). *The changing teaching environment.* Washington, DC: Institute for Education Policy Studies.

Hare, D., & Heap, J. L. (2001a). *Teacher recruitment and retention strategies in the Midwest: Where are they and do they work?* Naperville, IL: North Central Regional Educational Laboratory.

Hare, D., & Heap, J. L. (2001b). *Effective teacher recruitment and retention strategies in the Midwest: Who is making use of them?* Naperville, IL: North Central Regional Educational Laboratory.

Hawley, W. D. (2000). Quality induction is crucial. *State Education Leader, 18*(2). Available: www.ecs.org/clearinghouse/11/87/1187.htm#Quality

Haycock, K. (1998). Good teaching matters. . . A lot. *Thinking K–16, 3*(2), 3–14. Available: www.edtrust.org/maindocuments/k16_summer98.pdf

Ingersoll, R. (1997). Teacher turnover and teacher quality: The recurring myth of teacher shortages. *Teachers College Record, 99*(1), 41–44.

Ingersoll, R. (1998). The problem of out-of-field teaching. *Phi Delta Kappan, 79*(10), 773–776.

Ingersoll, R. (2000). A different approach to solving the teacher shortage problem. *Policy Perspectives, 2*(2), 6, 8.

Ingersoll, R. (2001). Teacher turnover and teacher shortages. *American Educational Research Journal, 38*(3), 499–534.

Ingersoll, R. M., Alsalam, N., Quinn, P., & Bobbitt, S. (1997). *Teacher professionalization and teacher commitment: A multilevel analysis.* Washington, DC: National Center for Education Statistics.

Johnson, S. (2000). Teaching's next generation. *Education Week, 19*(39), 33, 48.

Johnson, S. M., Birkeland, S., Kardos, S. M., Kauffman, D., Liu, E., & Peske, H. G. (2001, July/August). Retaining the next generation of teachers: The importance of school-based support. *Harvard Education Letter, 6,* 8.

Kauffman, D., Johnson, S. M., Kardos, S. M., Liu, E., & Peske, H. G. (2001). "Lost at sea": New teachers' experiences with curriculum and assessment. Unpublished paper.

Liu, E., Kardos, S. M., Kauffman, D., Peske, H. G., & Johnson, S. M. (2000). *Barely breaking even: Incentives, rewards, and the high costs of choosing to teach.* Available: www.gse.harvard.edu/~ngt/Barely%20Breaking%20Even%200700.pdf

Lortie, D. (1975). *Schoolteacher: A sociological study.* Chicago: University of Chicago Press.

National Association of State Boards of Education (NASBE). (1998, October). *The numbers game: Ensuring quantity and quality in the teaching workforce*. Alexandria, VA: Author.

National Commission on Teaching and America's Future. (1996). *What matters most: Teaching for America's future*. New York: Author.

Olson, L., & Jerald, C. D. (1998). The challenges. In *Quality Counts '98: The Urban Challenge*. Available: www.edweek.org/sreports/qc98/index.htm

Prince, C. (2002). *The challenge of attracting good teachers and principals to struggling schools*. Arlington, VA: American Association of School Administrators.

Spring, J. (1996). *American education*. New York: McGraw-Hill.

U.S. Department of Education. (2000). *Eliminating barriers to improving teaching*. Washington, DC: Author.

Wayne, A. J. (2000). Teacher supply and demand: Surprises from primary research. *Education Policy Analysis Archives, 8*(47). Available: http://epaa.asu.edu/epaa/v8n47.html

2

Improving the Quality of the Teaching Force

A Conversation with David C. Berliner

Marge Scherer

Professor David C. Berliner began studying teacher expertise in 1977. His observations of extraordinary teachers had profound implications for teacher training. By contrasting the well-trained, confident expert with the beginner who received the worst placements and the least support in the classroom, he made a case for providing more field-based experiences and mentoring for teacher candidates and beginning teachers.

Berliner is the coauthor of The Manufactured Crisis: Myths, Fraud, and the Attack on America's Public Schools *(Addison-Wesley, 1995) and is Regents Professor of Psychology in Education at Arizona State University, Tempe, AZ 85287-0211. Here, he talks about the need for more highly trained teachers and offers recommendations for improving the profession for experts and beginners alike.*

This interview originally appeared in the May 2001 issue of Educational Leadership.

A few years ago, you wrote about the expert teacher and the qualities needed to be one. Are you still exploring that topic?

Yes, and we've verified that it takes between five to eight years to master the craft of teaching. Only through experiencing the complexity of the classroom does a teacher learn. We now know that we cannot completely pre-train teachers. A college degree in education only takes you so far. It prepares you to be a beginner in a complex world.

What expert teachers have is case knowledge. They can go back in their memory banks to compare situations and figure out what to do. When expert teachers encounter a new student, a new learning problem, or new curriculum materials, they have references stored in memory. Expert teachers are also much better at impromptu responses. They're much better at capturing teachable moments. They know what's going on in the classroom all the time. They know how to get the class from point A to point B. Novices have no such experiences stored in their memory banks. Of course, some novices never get a clue about what's going on; they never learn from experience. But promising teachers and experts are learning each year.

If so much must be learned through on-the-job experience, what is it that professional education and certification do to prepare teachers?

Professional education gives teachers more familiarity with cultural, academic, and human diversity. Methods courses teach the pedagogical side of algebraic equations or the rain cycle. In professional studies, teachers begin to probe the underlying ecology of learning, teaching, and assessment. Without a professional knowledge base, a teacher takes a lot longer to understand how students learn and what and how they need to be taught.

Imagine going into a hardware store and not knowing the names of the things you need to buy. Professional education teaches the vocabulary of schools—*learning disabled, gifted, mean, median, mode.* And it teaches the pedagogy: What does it mean to do reciprocal teaching? How does one teach math in a way that allows kids to discover the answers? Untrained teachers cannot invent reciprocal teaching on their own. Learning some tips about classroom management during a short-term summer program is not enough.

At a recent meeting about school choice, advocates of charter schools were arguing for fewer regulations concerning teacher certification. They want principals to be allowed to choose from bright candidates who are not necessarily certified. In these times of shortages, how do we convince the general public of the importance of trained teachers?

We disseminate the research that shows that uncertified teachers do not perform as well in the classroom as certified teachers. Experienced teachers have more skills than inexperienced teachers. That's why almost all the prestigious private schools hire certified teachers. It's only the poorest of the private schools that are hiring uncertified teachers. In Arizona, the five charter schools leading in achievement hire certified teachers.

In Phoenix, Arizona, candidates in Teach for America are having terrible difficulties in the schools. Our university is mentoring the entire group. The candidates are having difficulties because they have not had training, and it's very hard to teach in the settings in which we put them. I'm not a fan of Teach for America, but I'm not against it, either, because some districts have a real need for more teachers. But we shouldn't assume that these bright, uncertified teachers are competent. They're not.

What can schools do to attract a new generation of teachers—young people who have so many more high-paying options open to them?

One answer is better pay. In this culture, pay and status go hand in hand, and teachers are not well paid. Teachers don't have status in the eyes of some of their own students. Pay and status overlap, and we have to provide novice and experienced teachers with both.

In the United States, beginning teachers are earning about $8,000 a year less than other college-educated professionals.

In my state, a teacher starts at about $27,000. Graduates from the school of business start at $35,000. The business grads are no smarter than the education students. Their coursework is no harder. Why can't teachers start out $8,000 higher?

Why can't they?

If you look at purchasing power parities, 7 of 23 nations exceed the United States in starting salary for teachers. The richest nation in the world—the richest nation the world has ever seen—is the United States, and yet seven other nations are willing to start their teachers at a higher salary. Nine of 21 nations exceed the United States in salaries at the top of the schedule—the salary for a teacher at the end of his or her teaching career. Twelve nations invest more in education than the United States does. Those other nations are saying that education, educators, schools, and children are worth more to them. Let's be clear. The United States is saying to its educators that they are not really important. If we thought they were important, we'd pay them a larger share of our gross domestic product, as other nations do.

What can the profession itself do to improve the quality of teachers?

To improve our profession, we need a twofold approach. One is to improve salaries. Both starting salaries and top salaries need to be higher. The other is to improve teachers' working conditions. Teachers must become more involved in their own professional lives. Unless we start changing working conditions so that teachers participate more in planning the curriculum, choosing the tests, and running the schools, thoughtful professionals are going to bail out. The current emphasis on testing has already driven out people because it takes away characteristics that define for teachers what it means to be a professional.

Teachers and physicians practice an art. Currently, physicians determine what to accomplish during rounds, but imagine how they would react if the state told doctors how to do rounds. Just as we are seeing physicians leaving the field because insurance companies have taken away their freedom to practice medicine, we're seeing the same trend for teachers operating under an inappropriate use of testing. Some states are telling them, "This is what you teach, and this is how you teach it." So teachers are leaving.

When you say you'd like to see teachers more involved in the professional life of schools, what kind of involvement are you advocating?

I'm not talking so much about site-based management as about teachers studying one another's lessons the way the Japanese do—visiting classes, presenting case studies about hard-to-teach kids, advising one another. I'm talking about the involvement of teachers in the life of their schools, their communities, their kids, and the decisions about curriculum. Too many teachers show up at school in the morning and go home in the afternoon. They have nothing to do with the life of their school. They don't even live in the community.

What should schools do to attract more minority candidates into teaching?

Start where the minorities are—for example, in the community colleges. Increase pre-education coursework about education issues and policy, and explain to minority students what education can be as a profession. Education is a wonderful opportunity, especially for the first-generation college graduate. We need to systematically recruit minority candidates, not wait for them to show up.

Do required teacher tests increase the quality of the teaching force?

Nobody wants an incompetent teacher in the classroom, but the teacher tests are not always the best way to tell who is competent. Putting candidates in a classroom and evaluating them is a better way to determine competence. At the university level of teacher education, we do a pretty good job of policing ourselves. Nobody believes that we do, but we do. We require student teaching of all candidates. And each year, we recommend that some students not be certified by the state to teach.

But a time of shortage is the wrong time to come down with a heavy fist in the form of a teacher test. We need to open doors, not close them.

How serious a problem is out-of-field teaching?

The statistics about out-of-field teaching are shocking. Only 41 percent of those who teach math have a math degree. Out-of-field teaching is a tremendous problem for minority school districts and rural school districts. But it's not a problem for the wealthy school districts. There isn't a single uncertified teacher in one of our wealthy Phoenix districts, but there are 50 or 60 uncertified teachers in one of our poorest districts. And we have data that show that the uncertified teachers achieve less with students than the certified teachers do.

How do we solve this problem?

If you were running any business that has a shortage of employees, you would recruit and pay the candidates you need. Industry complains about out-of-field teachers, but industry is stealing our mathematicians. It has stolen one of the best and the brightest from the faculty of my university. We can't compete when industry doubles the salary.

What do you think about the career stage programs that allow teachers to advance from intern to novice to advanced levels, much as Cincinnati is implementing?

Career stages offer a mechanism for giving rewards to teachers and for devising ways that experienced teachers can nurture the next generation. The National Board for Professional Teaching Standards also provides a mechanism to give more remuneration to the best teachers. If districts use these programs wisely, they will provide a richer professional life for their teachers and increase the pay for the best of them.

We recently published several articles arguing the value of merit pay. Will merit pay improve the status of teachers and make them more accountable?

I'm not a confirmed advocate of merit pay, but I am an advocate of National Board certification, and that's a form of merit pay. Teachers who pass those rigorous requirements show that they're superior in their knowledge and abilities. They ought to be paid for that. Some states offer a $10,000-a-year raise to those who earn the certificate, and that is great.

But receiving merit pay on the basis of their students' performance could lead to teachers doing the wrong thing in their classroom. Under such conditions, you see cheating. You see a narrowing of the curriculum—all for a few hundred dollars more a year. We ought to avoid this kind of merit pay. As for accountability, I think we'll find that most of the rewards will go to affluent schools. Most of the punishments will go to the schools with the harder-to-teach kids. These systems are patently unfair.

What have been the most promising reforms for teacher education during the last 10 years?

The push to field-based programs has been helpful. Professional development schools and laboratory-type schools have taken education courses off campus, put university students in the elementary and high schools, and teamed classroom teachers and college professors. More of our students are learning how to teach in real schools than students did 15 years ago. That's a good trend, a healthy trend. The use of more clinical faculty is both fiscally smart for the university and good for the students. People rotate in, teach the course for a few years, and then go back to their original workplaces.

And mentoring has been an important reform. Mentoring programs are promising for two reasons. First, they cut the dropout rate of teachers from roughly 50 to 15 percent during the first five years of teaching. Mentoring is very important; without it, our shortages will grow.

But the second reason that we need mentoring is a moral, not a pragmatic, one. We must not abandon beginners who have been placed in the complex world of teaching. Through apprenticeships, novices can learn from masters. Mentoring helps new teachers think about their experience, and it helps them handle the emotional side of teaching. Teaching is an emotionally draining occupation. Teachers get caught up in the lives of the kids and their parents. They need to know what a healthy response is and when to put up boundaries. They need clear advice about how to do something better or different the next time they teach it.

How widespread is the practice of mentoring?

Not widespread enough. We have one of the largest programs here at Arizona State. We mentor more than 1,000 teachers in their first two years of teaching. About 300 teachers from the school districts mentor these new teachers and dozens of supervisors from the university are working in the schools. Every state really needs a program like this. It costs a few hundred dollars per teacher per year for the first two years of the teacher's professional life. But mentoring programs cut the dropout losses from the teaching profession, and they are morally the right thing to do.

How do we change the public's negative perception of teachers?

Only teachers themselves can change the public's perception of teachers. Teachers need to provide more leadership, to be more politically active, and to show that they are concerned about the community. They should share their intellectual skills with the public by writing op-ed pieces and letters to the editor and by speaking at public meetings. No one else can change the perception of teachers except teachers themselves, but there *are* three million of them. And they ought to be out there—and much more active than they are now.

Part II

Welcoming Teachers

3

Keeping New Teachers in Mind

Susan Moore Johnson and Susan M. Kardos

Susan Moore Johnson is the Carl H. Pforzheimer Jr. Professor of Education in Teaching and Learning and principal investigator for the Project on the Next Generation of Teachers at the Harvard Graduate School of Education. Susan M. Kardos is an advanced doctoral student and a research assistant for the Project on the Next Generation of Teachers. Both authors can be reached by e-mail at ngt@gse.harvard.edu.

This article originally appeared in the March 2002 issue of Educational Leadership.

Her first days teaching science in an inner-city middle school were awful, Laura recalled. She hadn't begun with high expectations for professional support—"I assumed that the teachers would be unsupportive, sort of that sink-or-swim mentality. . . . that I was all on my own, and that it was me or nothing," she said—yet she was still surprised by the lack of organized induction. When she attended the district's orientation meeting for all new teachers, she found nothing there to help her begin her work as a classroom teacher. A day had been set aside when "we were supposed to come to our schools and get oriented," but Laura's principal "didn't do anything." In fact, Laura only learned which classes she would teach when she received the schedule at a faculty meeting the day before school started.

In an effort to understand new teachers' experiences and determine best practices in teacher recruitment, support, and retention, the Project on the Next Generation of Teachers at the Harvard Graduate School of Education is conducting a five-year, qualitative study of 50 new Massachusetts teachers.[1] Results from the first phase of the study, in which Project staff interviewed first- and second-year teachers in diverse school settings, indicate that, unfortunately, Laura's experience is not unusual.

Esther, a former engineer in the space industry, came to teaching through an alternative certification program. She described her district's orientation program for new teachers as "an indoctrination to the district, to the union. We got all that stuff. They talked about benefits and health care." But at her school site—where she would succeed or fail with her students—there was nothing: "Here it's pretty much, 'There's your classroom. Here's your book. Good luck.'"

Robert was similarly dismayed as he prepared for the opening of school and his first day as a new teacher. He had come to teaching after 30 years as a lawyer, having recently earned a master's degree and teaching certificate from a traditional teacher education program. When he was informed about the school's formal orientation meetings, he thought, "Wonderful. They'll introduce me to everything. I'll know what's going on." He had hoped to learn about the school, his colleagues, the school's technology, and anything else he might need to know to do his job well. Instead, he said he got "none of that," only a series of meetings about general topics, without any focus on "the way [this school] actually does things." He said flatly that it was "a joke."

Some new teachers were warmly welcomed in their schools, introduced to their colleagues, and provided with information about the classes that they would teach. Very few, however, were engaged in discussions about the pressing, school-specific questions of curriculum, instruction, and classroom management that most concern new teachers: What is expected of them at this school? What can they expect from their students? Which teaching strategies work? Which don't? What curriculum and books should they use? How should they organize their classrooms or their grade books? How will they know if their students are learning what they're trying to teach?

Laura was assigned a mentor who might have helped her answer such questions over time. He taught a different grade and subject, however, and

---

[1] The Project on the Next Generation of Teachers at the Harvard Graduate School of Education addresses issues related to attracting, supporting, and retaining new teachers. Directed by Susan Moore Johnson and funded by the Spencer Foundation, the Project team also includes Sarah Birkeland, Susan M. Kardos, David Kauffman, Edward Liu, and Heather G. Peske. For more information about the Project, please visit www.gse.harvard.edu/~ngt. For a full account of the Project study, see Kardos, Johnson, Peske, Kauffman, and Liu (2001).

they met "zero times." Many new teachers in our study went through their first months of school believing that they should already know how their schools work, what their students need, and how to teach well. When they had questions about their schools and their students, they eavesdropped on lunchroom conversations and peered through classroom doors seeking clues to expert practice. Having no access to clear answers or alternative models compromised the quality of their teaching, challenged their sense of professional competence, and ultimately caused them to question their choice of teaching as a career.

Wanted: School-Based Professional Development

Unfortunately, the mismatch between the needs of these new teachers and the support they received reflects the experiences of countless new teachers across the United States. The questions and uncertainty that new teachers bring to school require far more than orientation meetings, a mentor in the building, directions to the supply closet, and a written copy of the school's discipline policy. What new teachers want in their induction is experienced colleagues who will take their daily dilemmas seriously, watch them teach and provide feedback, help them develop instructional strategies, model skilled teaching, and share insights about students' work and lives. What new teachers need is sustained, school-based professional development—guided by expert colleagues, responsive to their teaching, and continual throughout their early years in the classroom. Principals and teacher leaders have the largest roles to play in fostering such experiences.

Diverse Paths to Teaching

The variety in backgrounds of today's new teachers increases the importance of providing useful and sustained professional development at the school site. The current teacher shortage and changes in certification requirements in many states have led schools to hire teachers with varying degrees of preparation. Many novices have completed traditional teacher education programs that include extensive coursework and student teaching. Some have completed full-year internships with master teachers in professional development schools. Still others are entering teaching through alternative certification programs that have only a summer component, which includes both coursework and practice teaching. Finally, an increasing number of entrants with no preparation at all take on full-time teaching assignments with emergency certificates.

The new teachers in our study who attended only summer preparation components reported feeling unprepared to teach, but they were not alone in their expressed need for ongoing school-site induction and support. We found that the daily, complicated demands of teaching left even those teachers who had extensive preservice training wanting more. They yearned for school-site support and professional development as they chose and adapted curriculums, planned and implemented lessons, and managed classrooms.

New teachers also enter the field at different points in their professional careers. The current cohort of new teachers includes both the 22-year-olds entering teaching as a first career, and the midcareer switchers who have left what they found to be unfulfilling work in such careers as sales, law, or engineering. Our survey of a random sample of new teachers in New Jersey indicated that 46 percent were career changers who were, on average, 35 years old. We also found that, in New Jersey, more midcareer entrants than first-career teachers came to teaching through such abbreviated routes as alternative certification programs. These midcareer switchers often bring to the classroom strong subject-matter competence and mature job skills, but they lack knowledge about and experience with students, curriculum, pedagogy, and the daily routines of schools.

The Importance of a School's Professional Culture

Most of the new teachers we interviewed hoped to find support and guidance in their schools, but some were more fortunate than others in entering environments that better addressed their needs. To learn about the assistance they received, we asked teachers about their interactions with their colleagues and their principals. When did they meet? What did they talk about? Where did they go for help or ideas about what to teach? Did they have a mentor? If so, how often did they interact, and what did they discuss with the mentor? Had someone observed them teach, and did they receive helpful feedback? As our respondents described their interactions with colleagues in their schools, clusters, departments, or teams, three types of professional culture emerged.

Veteran-Oriented Professional Cultures

Some teachers found themselves in what we called *veteran-oriented professional cultures*, where the modes and norms of professional practice are determined by, and aimed to serve, veteran faculty members. According to the new teachers, these schools, or subunits within schools, typically had a high proportion of veteran teachers with well-established, independent patterns of work. Sometimes collegial interactions were cordial in such settings; sometimes they were cold.

Regardless of the tenor of teacher interaction, these schools were not organized to engage new teachers or to acquaint them with expert practice. New teachers who experienced veteran-oriented cultures in their schools generally remained on the margins, without induction into the professional life of the school. Respondents often said that veteran teachers were highly skilled, but new teachers, who might work across the hall from those veterans, had no access to that expertise.

Such was 22-year-old Katie's experience in her new elementary school. She was clear about what she thought would be "the best kind of support for a first-year teacher": "Someone to meet with regularly to just talk about anything and everything, what's going on in your room; someone who can come in and observe you and make practical suggestions." Katie found herself isolated from her veteran colleagues, who seemed to know how to teach. Despite the high skill and good intentions of her first mentor, Katie did not get what she knew she needed: "I'm very isolated from her. . . . I met with her a few times and I was always welcome to go in her room and take a look at her materials and borrow anything that she had. But she just didn't have the time to come in and observe me and really talk with me practically about the things that I could do in here."

Novice-Oriented Professional Cultures

Other new teachers described working in what we labeled *novice-oriented professional cultures*, where youth, inexperience, and idealism prevailed. These school sites generally included two types of schools: start-up charter schools staffed largely with new recruits, many of whom had no formal preparation as teachers; and urban schools that were poorly organized or in disrepair, and experienced high turnover as teachers left for better work settings. In these schools, with so many new teachers, there existed an abundance of energy and vigorous commitment—but little professional guidance about how to teach.

Gwen, a 23-year-old novice teacher, taught in an urban school where most of her colleagues were close to her age and also new teachers: "So it was really difficult last year. And there was no set way of doing things. Everything was just kind of up in the air. It was chaos." She and her colleagues had no access to experienced teachers to help guide them in their difficult work. Although she acknowledged that things began to get better in her second year, she explained that, in her first year, "we felt like we were just kind of drifting along in our own little boat."

Integrated Professional Cultures

Finally, there were teachers who were fortunate to begin their teaching careers in what we called *integrated professional cultures*. These schools, or sub-units within schools, encouraged ongoing professional exchange across experience levels and sustained support and development for all teachers. Such schools did not endorse separate camps of veterans and novices; rather, teamwork and camaraderie distinguished these work settings.

New teachers in schools with integrated professional cultures believed that their expert colleagues not only understood the importance of mentoring, but also benefited from the mentoring relationship. New teachers who found themselves in such schools seemed to be better served—and thus, more able to serve their students. In addition, initial evidence from our longitudinal study suggests that new teachers working in settings with integrated professional cultures remained in their schools and in public school teaching in higher proportions than did their counterparts in veteran-oriented or novice-oriented professional cultures. In other words, the professional culture of schools may well affect teacher retention over the long term.

Laura had been assigned to work with a cluster of 7th grade teachers who served 110 students. Working together, that cluster of teachers developed an integrated professional culture. The school schedule provided a daily block of time when they could meet to discuss their students and coordinate what they would teach and how they would teach it. Laura's new colleagues in the cluster had 4–14 years of experience, and fortunately for her, they were eager to share what they knew.

After the second week of school, when two of her colleagues saw Laura in tears after she had walked students out at the end of the day, "They circled me and brought me up [to the classroom]. . . . They said, 'OK, this is what you have to do.' And that's when [my cluster leader] taught two of my classes. . . . They took me under their wings and just said, 'OK, here are some very specific things you can do.'"

The cluster leader, who taught in the room next to Laura's, had just been certified as an accomplished teacher by the National Board for Professional Teaching Standards. When she realized that Laura's mentoring experience was inadequate, she stepped in, meeting with Laura daily at lunch, watching her teach, and modeling effective classroom management strategies.

Laura credits her colleagues in the cluster with helping her gain the skills and confidence to continue teaching: "Without them, I wouldn't be here. There is no way. I wouldn't have survived. . . . After the first three days of school, I couldn't see how it could ever work."

At the end of the first semester, she reported, "I feel supported, and I feel like people listen to my ideas."

The Importance of Organized Support

Neither conventional inservice training, with its intermittent after-school sessions dealing with such generic issues as student services or assessment policies, nor the periodic visits of the school district's curriculum coordinators or academic coaches to new teachers' classrooms are enough to meet teachers' ongoing needs. Laura received more than just moral support from her colleagues: Structures were in place that enabled the teachers in her cluster to plan lessons and discuss students together, to visit one another's classes, and to hone their teaching skills together.

On-Site and On-Time Professional Development

Schools must provide new teachers with on-site professional development and make sure that new teachers have access to help on short notice when a lesson goes awry, a student is not responding to the new teacher's repertoire of teaching strategies, or a parent requires an immediate conference. New teachers need mentors who have time to observe and offer advice, or a small team of colleagues that they can convene for help on short notice.

Effective Principals

New teachers who found themselves in integrated professional cultures described their principals as visibly engaged in both the daily life of the school and the professional work of the teachers. These principals focused on the improvement of teaching and learning, visited classrooms, and provided feedback. They arranged school schedules so that expert teachers could teach model lessons or meet with new teachers one-on-one or in small groups. They helped teachers set priorities in their professional goals, recommended conferences or institutes that teachers might attend, and cultivated a professional culture in which teachers were collectively responsible for student and teacher learning.

Teacher Leaders

The practical, ongoing support that new teachers received from experienced colleagues in integrated cultures indicates that teacher leaders also have crucial roles to play. For example, veteran teachers might serve as mentoring coordinators, model teachers, team leaders, and in-class coaches. Schools can draw on the expertise and leadership of teachers certified by the National Board for Professional Teaching Standards, as Laura's school did.

New teachers flourish in an integrated professional culture that encourages teacher collaboration across experience levels, but veteran teachers also benefit from such professional exchange. In addition to the obvious rewards of mentoring for both parties, new teachers often possess skills—such as integrating technology into the curriculum or interpreting data from standards-based assessments—that veteran teachers need. Schools that gear professional development to both the ongoing induction of new teachers, and the continual renewal of veteran teachers, serve all educators well—thereby enabling them to serve all their students well.

4

The Principal's Role in New Teacher Induction

Cynthia L. Carver

Cynthia L. Carver is an assistant professor in the Department of Teaching, Learning, and Leadership, Western Michigan University, 2437 Sangren Hall, Kalamazoo, MI 49009. She can be reached by phone at (269) 387-1722 and by e-mail at cynthia.carver@wmich.edu.

Each time a teacher resigns, the hiring process must begin anew. While veteran teachers lament or applaud the loss of a colleague, the building principal posts a job opening and assembles a hiring team in hopes of securing the most able candidate. As summer fades and the new school year approaches, veteran staff members will join forces with the principal to orient the replacement, assign a mentor, and shuffle scarce resources so that the newcomer feels welcomed and equipped to start the year. If everything goes well, the new teacher will eventually become a full and contributing member of the staff. But in too many cases, the newcomer will resign in the next year or two, and the scenario will repeat itself.

Research has found that large proportions of new teachers leave the profession within their first three to five years, just as they are getting their professional feet wet (Darling-Hammond, 1997). Many find the job impossible and the demands too great. Many new teachers leave the profession because of poor working conditions, including low pay and status. Others leave because of a lack of support from administrators, colleagues, students, and parents (Ingersoll, 2001).

Public concern over alarming new teacher attrition and retention rates has helped fuel widespread interest in formal induction programs. Policymakers see induction as a possible solution to multiple problems: a way to improve teaching, raise retention rates, eliminate the unfit, and increase student achievement (Fideler & Haselkorn, 1999; Huling-Austin, 1990).

Traditionally, discussions of teacher induction have not considered the role of the school principal (Zeichner & Gore, 1990). Researchers and experts typically limit their recommendations for principal support of induction to program advocacy and beginning-of-the-year orientations (Brock & Grady, 2001). But principals at least have the responsibility of evaluating new teachers and fostering workplace conditions that support their development. Shouldn't principals play a larger role in supporting beginning teachers?

Core Induction Tasks for Principals

To better understand what effective principals do to support, develop, and assess their newest teachers, I followed four elementary principals—each of whose schools operated a highly regarded induction program—for three years (Carver, 2002). Drawing on their work, I identified a set of core tasks through which principals can support novice teachers (see Figure 4.1). These include recruiting, hiring, and placing new teachers; providing orientation to the site and resource assistance; managing the school environment; building relationships between principals and teachers; providing leadership for instructional development through formative and summative evaluation; and facilitating a supportive school context.[1]

None of the four principals considered new teacher support to be an added aspect of their work. Rather, they incorporated various combinations of these strategies willingly and naturally into their daily routines. Supporting new teachers was simply part of the job.

New Teacher Recruiting, Hiring, and Placing

Effective principals recruit aggressively and then streamline the hiring process so that novices are quickly brought on board and have a chance to settle in before the school year begins. After new teachers are hired, effective principals make sure to place them in their areas of expertise and licensure,

[1] These core principal support tasks have wide support in the literature. For examples, see Brock and Grady (2001); Darling-Hammond, Berry, Haselkorn, and Fideler (1999); Donaldson and Poon (1999); Fideler and Haselkorn (1999); National Commission on Teaching and America's Future (1996); Odell and Huling (2000); Portner (2001); and Villani (2002).

FIGURE 4.1
Core Tasks for Principals in Supporting New Teachers

Recruiting, Hiring, and Placing New Teachers

- Recruit aggressively; streamline and facilitate the hiring process
- Hire early so that the novices can settle in
- Assign novices to subject areas and grade levels for which they are qualified
- Secure classroom placements that optimize the novices' chance for success
- Distribute challenging students among classrooms
- Protect novices' time by limiting extra duties and responsibilities

Providing Site Orientation and Resource Assistance

- Facilitate introduction and welcome to the site
- Offer site orientation to highlight available resources, procedures, and policies
- Assign in-building mentors (if not already provided)
- Provide needed resources and supplies

Managing the School Environment

- Clearly articulate expectations for teachers
- Streamline state and district paperwork
- Protect novices from the competing demands of state and district mandates
- Maintain a disciplined school environment

Building Relationships Between Principals and Teachers

- Maintain regular personal communication with the novice
- Acknowledge and reward performance, as appropriate
- Maintain an open-door policy; ask how you can be helpful

Fostering Instructional Development Through Formative Assessment

- Facilitate novices' participation in professional development opportunities
- Provide opportunities and incentives for all teachers to work together
- Provide opportunities for novices to gather and work together
- Protect planning time for novices
- Visit novices' classrooms and provide feedback; help novices set reasonable goals
- Review lesson plans; offer instruction in teaching strategies

---

FIGURE 4.1 (*continued*)

Core Tasks for Principals in Supporting New Teachers

- Facilitate novices' observation of other teachers
- Engage in ongoing professional dialogue with novices

Providing Formative and Summative Evaluation

- Explain expectations and procedures at the beginning of the year
- Schedule observations in advance; provide novices with copies of evaluation records
- Use standards to guide your assessment
- Be positive but honest in your feedback; recognize novices as beginners
- Help novices set reasonable goals for their learning and development
- Balance formal observations and conferences with informal observations and feedback
- Coordinate evaluation activities with induction and mentoring program

Facilitating a Supportive School Context

- Foster a welcoming, nurturing, and collegial work environment that values critical inquiry, reflection, and risk taking
- Help other teachers understand and acknowledge novices' development and needs
- Set high expectations for teaching and learning and make them clear to all
- Use teaching standards to structure professional development opportunities
- Model collaborative working behavior

---

provide them with adequate resources to meet their needs, and assign them only limited extra duties and responsibilities to optimize their chance of success. In the words of one principal, "I really want them to focus on their teaching the first year. I don't want to distract them from that because they form their habits so early in their careers. I want them to concentrate on improving the quality of their teaching." To protect the novice's time, this principal takes care to limit the number of new teacher committee assignments to two: one requiring a light commitment and a second requiring a medium commitment.

Providing Site Orientation and Resource Assistance

After they are hired and placed, new teachers need to become acquainted with the way their new school does things. Principals can help meet this need by sponsoring a building-level orientation at the opening of the school year to review key policies and procedures. In addition, principals may assign mentor or buddy teachers, thereby establishing a formal network of support for the novice. Principals can also help the new teacher obtain needed resources and supplies. As the year unfolds, effective principals tailor their actions to meet the individual needs of new teachers. As one principal said:

> It's the nuts and bolts. What do the teachers need so that they can do their job? Basic information about how the school works, the ins and outs, all the things that even as a student teacher you may not have been aware of, but that an experienced teacher takes for granted. We have an understanding that a lot of those pieces are missing and they need to be developed for that first-year teacher, so we try to be sensitive to that and support people and get those pieces in place.

Managing the School Environment

New teachers find it reassuring to know that their principal can be trusted to physically maintain the building and hold students accountable for acting in a responsible manner. Principals who facilitate a disciplined and orderly school environment enable the new teacher to concentrate on teaching students, rather than just managing them.

Principals can also help keep the new teacher's focus on teaching by streamlining such routine administrative tasks as the completion of state and district reports. For example, one principal passes on to the new teacher only those administrative requests that cannot be filled by office staff. In her words, "My vested interest is that new teachers do their job with as little disruption and as little confusion as possible."

Building Relationships Between Principals and Teachers

Although principals are busy people, it is important that they take time to get to know the new teachers in their school and establish working relationships with them—for example, by welcoming new teachers to the site, maintaining an open-door policy, being available for individual conferences, and attending to new teachers' real and perceived needs. The key is to facilitate a professional relationship between the novice and principal, as well as among peers throughout the system. Doing so opens the door to deeper and more substantive conversations, as noted by the principal who said:

> I'll ask about their families. I'll ask them about their kids. I develop a strong relationship with them. They know that I care about them as people. That relationship takes us a long way. It really opens the door for me to talk to them about superior performance.

Establishing a strong working relationship is particularly important when concerns arise about a new teacher's performance. As one principal said:

> When you have a comfortable relationship with a person, you can coach that person. So I am really conscious of building relationships with people so that they can be open to feedback. Without a rapport, it is hard to work with people, especially when you have concerns.

Providing Formative and Summative Assessment

Even when a school uses mentors, principals can play a significant role in promoting new teachers' development. Effective principals provide formative assessment by regularly visiting classrooms, reviewing lesson plans, and providing immediate feedback to their new teachers. They clearly express performance expectations, help novices set reasonable goals, and routinely engage in "pedagogical talk" with their teachers.

During the summative evaluation process, effective principals communicate their expectations clearly to the novice, focus their observations around the new teacher's explicit needs, and approach the process as trusted colleagues. Effective principals also coordinate evaluation activities with induction and mentoring programs to prevent unnecessary overlap or conflicting expectations. As one principal remarked, the process of conducting new teacher evaluations, including communication with the new teacher's mentor, actually helps her focus on new teachers' needs: "I don't like putting in the time, but it makes me think about each individual teacher, what is special about them, and their strengths and weaknesses . . . so it gets me to focus in."

Less visible, but equally important, effective principals encourage novices to work with other teachers to develop their instructional skills, through coplanning and coteaching, for example, or through observing in veteran teachers' classrooms. As one principal noted, "I encourage people to visit one another. I really facilitate opportunities for people to share things that are happening."

Facilitating a Supportive School Context

Of all the efforts effective principals undertake to support new teachers, building and sustaining a supportive school culture may be the most elusive. All teachers benefit from pleasant and collegial work environments, professional standards, and the development of a shared language around a common mission. Above all, the principal needs to establish high expectations for both student learning and teacher learning. In the words of one principal, "You start with making teachers feel good about themselves and what they are doing. Make them feel that this is a safe, risk-free environment for teaching and learning. If you set that up and do it consciously, they are going to do the work that they are about, which is intellectual."

The Little Things Add Up

Although principals can support, develop, and evaluate new teachers in countless ways, no principal in this study came close to doing it all. Rather, they reported picking and choosing among various alternatives, basing their decision on at least three things: the stated or perceived learning needs of the novice; the availability of school-based resources, both human and material; and their own skills and preferences as leaders.

The principal's role in supporting new teachers is therefore likely to shift with changing needs, interests, and contexts. For example, the principal may provide an orientation for all new teachers at the beginning of the academic year, but take different actions to support individual teachers as the school year progresses. He or she may encourage a young teacher struggling with classroom management to attend a seminar on the topic and give the teacher release time to observe in the classroom of his or her mentor. To help a new teacher who has an especially challenging set of students, the principal may assign a classroom assistant for part of the day.

Whatever specific actions principals decide to take, it's important that they demonstrate their care and concern. Gestures, large and small, add up. This is particularly true when the principal's actions are immediately visible. The novice teacher benefits when the principal quietly asks a colleague next door to keep an eye on the classroom, but gains even more if the principal personally observes in the classroom and offers counseling and advice.

District-Level Leadership

Principals have a critical role to play in new teacher support, development, and assessment. However, building capacity for that work rightfully rests on the shoulders of school district leadership. If school districts are serious about retaining new teachers, they need to encourage and support principal development in this area. They should expect principals to publicly articulate support for new teacher induction and mentoring and demonstrate visible on-site support for program work and activities. In addition, districts should encourage their principals to participate in program development and evaluation, including the selection and coordination of mentors.

To do this important work, principals must be knowledgeable about induction program goals and activities. They need to demonstrate an understanding of mentors' work with new teachers, including a healthy respect for mentor-novice confidentiality, and they need to become more aware of new teacher development and learning needs. School districts should provide meaningful professional development opportunities for principals that are focused on the effective practice of new teacher support, development, and assessment.

References

Brock, B. L., & Grady, M. L. (2001). *From first-year to first-rate: Principals guiding beginning teachers* (2nd ed.). Thousand Oaks, CA: Corwin.

Carver, C. L. (2002). *Principals' supporting role in new teacher induction.* Unpublished doctoral dissertation, Michigan State University, East Lansing.

Darling-Hammond, L. (1997). *Doing what matters most: Investing in quality teaching.* Kutztown, PA: National Commission on Teaching and America's Future.

Darling-Hammond, L., Berry, B. T., Haselkorn, D., & Fideler, E. (1999). Teacher recruitment, selection and induction: Policy influences on the supply and quality of teachers. In L. Darling-Hammond & G. Sykes (Eds.), *Teaching as the learning profession* (pp. 182–232). San Francisco: Jossey-Bass.

Donaldson, M. L., & Poon, B. (1999). *Reflections of first-year teachers on school culture: Questions, hopes, and challenges.* New Directions for School Leadership Series, Vol. 11, sponsored by the International Network of Principals' Centers. San Francisco: Jossey-Bass.

Fideler, E. F., & Haselkorn, D. (1999). *Learning the ropes: Urban teacher induction programs and practices in the United States.* Belmont, MA: Recruiting New Teachers.

Huling-Austin, L. (1990). Teacher induction programs and internships. In W. R. Houston, M. Haberman, & J. Sikula (Eds.), *Handbook of research on teacher education* (pp. 535–548). New York: Macmillan.

Ingersoll, R. M. (2001). Teacher turnover and teacher shortages. *American Educational Research Journal, 38*(3), 499–534.

Kardos, S. M., Johnson, S. M., Peske, H. G., Kauffman, D., & Liu, E. (2001, April). Counting on colleagues: New teachers encounter the professional culture of their schools. *Educational Administration Quarterly.*

National Commission on Teaching and America's Future. (1996). *What matters most: Teaching for America's future.* New York: Author.

Odell, S. J., & Huling, L. (2000). *Quality mentoring for novice teachers.* Washington, DC & Indianapolis, IN: Association of Teacher Educators and Kappa Delta Phi.

Portner, H. (2001). *Training mentors is not enough: Everything else schools and districts need to do.* Thousand Oaks, CA: Corwin.

Villani, S. (2002). *Mentoring programs for new teachers: Models of induction and support.* Thousand Oaks, CA: Corwin.

Zeichner, K. M., & Gore, J. M. (1990). Teacher socialization. In W. R. Houston, M. Haberman, & J. Sikula (Eds.), *Handbook of research on teacher education* (pp. 329–348). New York: Macmillan.

5

Induction Programs That Keep Working

Harry K. Wong

Harry K. Wong is a former high school science teacher. He is the coauthor with Annette Breaux of New Teacher Induction: How to Train, Support, and Retain New Teachers *(Performance Learning Systems, 2003), and can be reached by e-mail at harrykrose@aol.com.*

> In elementary school, no one ever picked me. That rejection and its resulting hurt stayed with me through life. So when I became a teacher, I vowed never to allow my students to be rejected. But how could I do that when rejection was the initial experience I encountered on my very first day as a new teacher? I was not introduced to the staff. I was not shown to my room. I was not told how to get supplies. I was not told how I would fit in and how I could contribute. I was not even shown the bathrooms! I left after my first year. Looking back, the reason is obvious. There was no culture at this school, so I could not fit in to something that did not exist. It was simply a place where people worked behind closed doors.

This story and many others like it have been shared with me over the years as I crisscross the country working with teachers.

The Most Significant Process

Research suggests that the most academically talented teachers leave in the greatest numbers. In a study from the North Central Regional Education Laboratory (Hare & Heap, 2001), a majority of superintendents in the region indicated that 75 to 100 percent of the teachers leaving the profession were "effective" or "very effective" in the classroom. Why did these capable teachers leave?

People crave connection. New teachers want more than a job: They want hope. They want to contribute to a group. They want to make a difference.

Belonging, a basic human need, provides the key to keeping skilled teachers. Structured, intensive induction programs can provide the connection teachers need—if these programs are built around sustained professional development within a learning community that treats new and veteran teachers with respect and that values their contributions.

Because new teachers want to be part of a team and part of a culture, the induction process should immerse them in the district's culture and unite them with everyone in the district as a cohesive, supportive instructional team. Under these conditions, new teachers quickly become a part of the district's "family."

Induction Programs That Provide Ongoing Learning

Induction is the process of preparing, supporting, and retaining new teachers. It includes all the things done to support new teachers and to acculturate them to teaching. Strong induction programs introduce new teachers to the responsibilities, missions, and philosophies of their schools, and treat teachers as lifelong learners from their very first day of teaching. The following three school districts and one school have highly successful new teacher induction programs. Their results speak volumes.

Newport-Mesa Schools, California

Christina Jurenko, director of Newport-Mesa's induction program, reports that the annual retention rate of new teachers was 85 percent in 1997. After the district installed a two-year induction program patterned after California's Beginning Teacher Support and Assessment model, the retention rate increased to 97 percent.

Sustained professional development is the method used in this induction program. The district fosters an atmosphere in which teachers want to learn and continue to grow as professionals. It sponsors teachers who want to attend conferences but requires that new teachers, veteran teachers, and administrators attend in groups to support the district's focus on teamwork.

The district encourages site administrators to organize study groups of learning teams on campus. These structures provide the type of organizational support that results in teacher learning. Teachers meet weekly in pairs and triads to reflect on practice, analyze student work, and study the impact of teaching on student growth. Networking, conducting case studies, coaching, creating teacher portfolios, and shadowing students are just a few of the techniques that study groups use to facilitate and sustain teacher growth and effectiveness.

Lafourche Parish Schools, Louisiana

Gary Babin, superintendent of Lafourche Parish, observes that in his district, "new teachers became highly successful and all were coming back the following year. This had never happened until we implemented an induction program."

New teachers in the district meet frequently: four days in early August with the induction team, which includes three curriculum coordinators and one principal; one day in late August with the three curriculum coordinators; once a month on-site with their facilitators; once a month at the district level with their support group; and weekly with their mentors. They participate in ongoing observations all year. They observe their mentors, and their mentors, administrators, curriculum facilitators, and curriculum coordinators observe them. They have two more days of meetings in January to prepare them for the Louisiana State Assessment that all new teachers in the state must pass during their third semester of teaching in order to receive certification. In addition, they meet for another full day in April for an induction review conducted by the three curriculum coordinators, in which new teachers share their first-year successes and receive further training in anticipation of their second year.

These support activities focus on establishing good classroom management; implementing basic, proven instructional strategies; and meeting the requirements set by the Louisiana Components of Effective Teaching. In addition, new teachers write professional development plans during their second semester of teaching, with the help of their mentors and administrators. These plans determine the kinds of ongoing individual help the new teachers receive from veteran teachers in their school.

The benefits of all these activities are clear. Lafourche retained 45 out of 46 new teachers hired in 2001–2002. More than 99 percent of the new teachers who have participated in the district's induction program have successfully completed state teacher certification requirements. The Louisiana Department of Education has adopted the Lafourche induction program as the model for the entire state.

Islip Public Schools, New York

Linda Lippman, the director of human resources and of the new teacher induction program for Islip Schools in New York, has the dual responsibility of training the teachers she hires. Her efforts have paid off. In the 1998–1999 school year, before Islip installed a formal induction program, the district retained only 29 of the 46 new teachers hired. In the subsequent three school years from 1999 to 2002, when a formal, three-year teacher induction program was installed, the district retained 65 teachers of 68 hired.

As part of their contract, teachers in their first three years attend monthly 90-minute study group meetings after school. The teachers are divided into groups by years in the district and by grade level, elementary (K–5) or secondary (6–12). Study group activities, led by veteran teachers and district curriculum leaders, focus on building skills in such areas as parent-teacher conferences, classroom management, lesson plans, and cooperative discipline. Teachers network, work on team-building and problem-solving techniques, and participate in sharing sessions in which they "steal" ideas from one another.

As new teachers proceed through their three-year tenure-track program, team-building activities promote a sense of cohesion and belonging and help them build relationships in support groups. Collegial circles meet informally between formal monthly meetings. Social studies teacher John Christie says that at Islip, "the induction program allowed me to share new teacher concerns, realize I wasn't alone, and discover solutions in a collegial environment."

Islip's new teachers participate in a Web quest workshop that gives them the opportunity to tailor activities to their respective education settings. The outcome is enriched curriculum activities and highly motivated adult learners. Workshop leaders model exemplary lessons and add to the new teachers' growing knowledge base.

Goldfarb Elementary School, Nevada

The best induction programs are sustained, on-site, and on time (Johnson & Kardos, 2002). Goldfarb Elementary School in Las Vegas, Nevada, typifies such a program. For the past six years, the school has enjoyed a 100 percent retention rate.

Goldfarb Elementary School builds on Clark County School District's three-year induction and training program, which includes such activities as an orientation program prior to the beginning of the school year; a Community Day at a mall sponsored by local businesses; a teaching strategy resource manual, *Great Beginnings;* monthly training sessions in everything from classroom management to lesson delivery; a teacher-training cadre available for training and assistance; on-site mentor-facilitators; monthly newsletters; new-teacher socials; and intranet services. A cadre of administrators and teachers oversees the induction program.

Training varies from year to year, depending on how many new teachers are hired, but it typically includes meeting three days before school begins for a dialogue on schoolwide procedures and expectations, and attending as many as 24 meetings during the school year for training on such topics as technology, balanced literacy, effective math lessons, Accelerated Schools, and guided reading.

Goldfarb Elementary School is a learning community—a place where teachers and administrators study, work, and learn together with the mission of improving student achievement. The school no longer uses mentors (Wong & Wong, 2002). Instead, the administration conducts a survey to determine the needs of student teachers and new teachers and publicizes the list. "Tons" of experienced teachers respond with offers to answer questions, help with problems, or present information at in-house training sessions. In this true learning community of educators committed to sharing with and helping fellow educators on a sustained basis, new teachers believe that they can contribute and make a difference.

Induction Means More Than Mentoring

Induction and mentoring are not the same. Induction entails much more than connecting the novice with a veteran teacher—it is an organized, sustained, multiyear program structured by a school or district. Induction is a group process that organizes the expertise of educators within the shared values of a culture, whereas mentoring is a one-on-one process concerned with supporting individual teachers.

It takes five to seven years to develop an effective teacher. A mentor may help in a neophyte teacher's first year or two, but professional development should continue throughout the teacher's career. Therefore, we must stop trying to portray mentoring as an effective stand-alone method for supporting and retaining teachers.

After 20 years of experimenting with mentoring as a process for helping new teachers, researchers have produced few comprehensive studies to validate its effectiveness (Feiman-Nemser, 1996). The results of mentor programs may be uneven because in too many instances, the mentor is simply a veteran teacher who has been haphazardly selected by the principal and assigned to a new teacher, resulting in a "blind date" (Saphier, Freedman, & Aschheim, 2001).

Mentors can offer important support for new teachers, but they must be carefully selected and highly trained, have a clear understanding of their purpose, and serve as contributing members of an overall comprehensive induction program. Prince George's County Schools in Maryland, the 19th-largest school district in the United States, provides 40 hours of training for the mentoring component of its three-year induction process.

Effective Professional Development

Both new and veteran teachers often feel isolated in their jobs and thirst for more opportunities to network, share, and collaborate with their peers. They want a culture that acknowledges, respects, and nurtures them as professionals. They want to be involved in decision-making and leadership in their schools. They want time to collaborate with their peers and reflect on their craft. They want more opportunities to enhance their knowledge and skills and to advance in their careers. And they want these opportunities to be available from the beginning to the end of their teaching careers.

An organized, sustained professional development program provides these opportunities, encouraging new teachers and veteran teaches to stay in a district. The best professional development programs allow teachers to observe others, to be observed by others, and to be part of groups in which teachers share together, grow together, and learn to respect one another's work. According to a national study conducted by Garet, Porter, Desmoine, Birman, and Yoon (2001), teachers learn more in teacher networks and study groups than with mentoring, and they gain more from longer, sustained, and intensive professional development programs than from shorter ones.

Thus, professional development programs will make the strongest contribution to training and retaining good teachers when they

- Have networks that create learning communities.
- Treat every colleague as a valuable contributor.
- Turn ownership of learning over to the learners in study groups.
- Create learning communities in which everyone, new teachers as well as veteran teachers, gains knowledge.
- Demonstrate that quality teaching becomes not just an individual, but also a group, responsibility.

The professional development department at Flowing Wells Schools in Tucson, Arizona, operates under the banner of the Institute for Teacher Renewal and Growth. The induction phase of the program takes the new teachers through three stages during the first three years, from *novice* in their first year, to *advanced beginner* in their second year, and then to *competent teacher* in their third year. At these stages, they learn such skills as classroom management, essential elements of instruction, reading strategies, task analysis, and learning styles.

Teachers then enter a four-year growth stage. Teachers grow from *proficient* in their fourth year to an *expert teacher* in their eighth year. During these years, they take such courses as peer coaching, attention deficit disorder, multiple intelligences, assistive technology, cognitive coaching, honoring diverse student needs, question/response patterns, alignment of curriculum with state standards, and current research topics. Finally, the teacher enters seamlessly into a veteran teacher renewal program that is a career-long process for all staff members in the district. This program may explain why Flowing Wells has produced 12 finalists for teachers of the year for the state of Arizona, more than any other school district in the state.

The Real Beneficiaries

Research consistently supports the need for systematic induction of new teachers and the ongoing professional development of all teachers. Hiebert, Gallimore, and Stigler (2002), who write about building and sustaining a professional knowledge base for teaching, point to a growing consensus that professional development yields the best results when it is long-term, school-based, collaborative, focused on student learning, and linked to the curriculum. When all new teachers participate in a structured and sustained induction process that treats them as lifelong learners, the real beneficiaries are the students who reap the rewards of skillful, knowledgeable, effective teachers.

References

Feiman-Nemser, S. (1996). *Teacher mentoring: A critical review.* Washington, DC: ERIC Clearinghouse on Teaching and Teacher Education. (ERIC Document Reproduction Service No. ED 397 060).

Garet, M., Porter, A., Desmoine, L., Birman, B., & Yoon, K. S. (2001). What makes professional development effective? *American Educational Research Journal, 38*(4), 915–946.

Hare, D., & Heap, J. (2001). *Effective teacher recruitment and retention strategies in the midwest.* Naperville, IL: North Central Regional Laboratory. Available: www.ncrel.org/policy/pubs/html/strategy/index.html

Hiebert, J., Gallimore, R., & Stigler, J. W. (2002). A knowledge base for the teaching profession: What would it look like and how can we get one? *Educational Researcher, 31*(5), 3–15.

Johnson, S. M., & Kardos, S. M. (2002). Keeping new teachers in mind. *Educational Leadership, 59*(6), 13–16.

Saphier, J., Freedman, S., & Aschheim, B. (2001). *Beyond mentoring: How to nurture, support, and retain new teachers.* Newton, MA: Teachers 21.

Wong, H. K., & Wong, R. T. (2002, January). A most effective school. *Teachers Net Gazette, 3*(1) [Online journal]. Available: http://teachers.net/gazette/JAN02/covera.html

6

Why One Year of Support Is Not Enough

Martha Daniels and Gale Boring

Martha Daniels (danielsm@eagle4.stark.k12.oh.us) and Gale Boring (boringg@eagle4.stark.k12.oh.us) are peer consultants for Plain Local Schools, 901 44th St., N.W., Canton, OH 44718.

Every licensed profession requires a period of internship for new personnel—except education. Instead of providing an internship, we often send fresh, bright-eyed, idealistic college graduates into a classroom (sometimes with our most difficult students), shut the door, and say, "Go to it!" We veterans all remember those initial years of doubt, insecurity, and occasional terror at facing students, knowing that we were responsible for their learning and well-being for at least six hours a day.

New teachers often face overwhelming challenges, and attrition rates are high. Twenty percent of newly hired teachers leave the profession within three years, and 10 percent leave within their first year. The attrition rate in some urban centers is even worse (Recruiting New Teachers, 1999).

But educators are beginning to make significant strides to improve the situation. Induction programs for novice teachers help them gain the experience and confidence that they need to be successful in the classroom and remain in the profession (Sweeny, 2000). In the combined suburban and urban area of Canton, Ohio, the Plain Local School District has developed a mentoring and peer consultant program to meet the specialized needs of not only newly hired personnel—novices and experienced teachers new to the district—but also teachers in their second to fifth years in the district, and veteran teachers who need to improve their instructional skills. As a school system serving 6,300 K–12 students—13 percent from minority backgrounds, 25 percent on free and reduced-price lunch programs, 8.5 percent identified as gifted, and 12.7 percent with special needs—the district decided to do all it could to develop a corps of 350 skilled teachers who are committed to the profession.

Nurturing Newly Hired Teachers

Novice teachers are usually excited to be in a classroom, but many of them soon feel overwhelmed by the isolation, expectations, challenges, and lack of support from colleagues and administrators (Recruiting New Teachers, 1999). Beginning teachers are often reluctant to ask for help lest they appear unprepared and incompetent to their colleagues (Galvez-Hjornevik, 1986), and only about 8 percent actually do seek assistance (Sweeny, 2000). By matching new teachers with trained master teachers, the Plain school system brings together the enthusiasm and experience needed to reach professional competency.

The purpose of the first year of induction is to nurture new teachers and give them a basic framework for implementing effective classroom instruction. Ohio law mandates that all newly hired teachers have an individual mentor teacher who helps the new teacher set up the classroom, establish classroom procedures, find resources and curriculum materials, prepare for the Praxis III licensure assessment, and become oriented to the school, district, and community. Our district also requires new teachers to observe several practicing teachers for eight hours during the school year and to discuss the observations with their mentors in reflective conferences.

Mentors for novice teachers. Our district's mentors receive an additional yearly stipend; 15 hours of training in strategies developed by the Vanderbilt Institute, which include reflective listening and coaching techniques to help new teachers assess their skills effectively (Evertson & Smithey, 1999); and training in instructional structures developed by the Pathwise Institute on such subjects as planning lessons, fostering a positive classroom environment, and establishing instructional procedures (Educational Testing Service, 2001). The mentor's one-year commitment includes working at least 45 hours with an entry-level teacher during the school year, with one release day to observe and confer with the novice teacher. The number of mentors depends on the number of entry-year teachers.

Peer consultants for experienced teachers new to the district. Peer consultants provide collegial support to experienced teachers who are new to the district. Teachers in the district who have already served as mentors can apply to become peer consultants, a position that involves a minimum commitment of three years and additional training in coaching, observation, and evaluation techniques. Our district currently has two full-time consultants and five part-time consultants.

These peer consultants share district expectations, school culture, and curriculum goals with the newly hired but experienced teachers to help ensure a smooth transition to teaching in the new district. Each peer consultant meets individually with newly hired teachers for three to six hours each month and conducts an individual classroom observation at least once a month. Depending on the newly hired teacher's needs, the peer consultants work with each individual for 40 to 75 hours a year. To provide this opportunity, the district arranges for substitute teachers during the newly hired teachers' meetings with their consultants.

Professional development sessions for all newly hired teachers. During their first year, all newly hired teachers attend six district professional development sessions that provide information on district programs, technology, literacy, assessments, curriculum instruction, dealing with at-risk students, parent conferencing, and the teachers association.

The district's peer consultants join the mentors in participating in the six professional development sessions required for newly hired teachers. Central-office staff, the lead mentor, full-time peer consultants, and district specialists conduct the programs. The consultants have also developed a lesson plan book that provides space for daily lesson plans and offers weekly tips on such topics as record keeping and classroom management. New teachers prize these lesson plan books.

Beyond the First Year

In 1997, school administrators and teachers association leaders agreed that one year of support was insufficient for developing knowledgeable and confident teachers. The district wanted to go beyond simply nurturing first-year teachers and develop higher expectations for teachers at all years of experience.

After a team of teacher leaders and administrators researched mentoring programs (Danielson, 1996; Sclan & Darling-Hammond, 1992), it developed the peer consultant position to provide support not only for experienced teachers who were new to the district, but also during teachers' second through fifth years of teaching and for some veteran teachers. Peer consultants observe the teachers' classes, share classroom management strategies, conduct reflective discussions, discuss instructional strategies, suggest methods for management and discipline, and listen to teachers' concerns. They work closely with teachers to improve the quality of instruction and to help them develop effective instructional materials.

Our two full-time consultants are master teachers who have been released from classroom responsibilities for at least three years and work with 15 to 20 teachers who are at any stage of their careers. These full-time consultants may act as mentors for novice teachers, and as peer consultants for veteran teachers who need to improve their instructional skills. The part-time consultants are master classroom teachers who each work with three or four teachers. These consultants have a full class assignment but receive release time each month and extended-time pay for additional hours beyond the contractual day.

How do peer consultants assist teachers in their classrooms? One consultant conferred with three 1st grade teachers who felt overwhelmed by the demands of the grade-level literacy program. The group met to discuss classroom organization, learning centers, writing workshops, and word study. The teachers reflected together and revised classroom strategies, including the content of learning centers and transitions between activities. The consultant led the discussion and provided ideas and resources.

In a secondary school, middle and high school teachers wanted to know more about designing assessments and rubrics for specific projects and assignments. A peer consultant worked with individual teachers to analyze assignment expectations, reflect on the goals of the projects, and determine indicators of success. Together, the peer consultant and individual teachers developed rubrics that identified criteria for the assignments, guided the students in their work, and allowed the teachers to modify the assignment for at-risk students while maintaining rigorous work expectations.

Several teachers were finding both day-by-day lesson planning and long-range planning overwhelming tasks. The consultant and the teachers worked together to examine the grade-level curriculum, plan the year's material, and determine a sequence for developing concepts and a pace of instruction that could meet all requirements in a timely manner.

Consultants have the time to develop friendships with the teachers on a professional and a personal level, and the mutual respect and trust that they develop allow for open discussion and reflection. As second-year teacher Amy DePew commented, "This program sets teachers up for success, not failure. The professional development seminars helped me realize that I was not the only one learning how to become a good teacher. It is a valuable, warm, and supportive experience."

Other certified staff members also see peer consultants as a valuable resource and seek them out for professional assistance and advice, which allows the consultant program to have an impact far beyond helping the district's newer teachers.

The consultant support can last up to five years, depending on the need of the individual employee. Teachers can request the assistance of a peer consultant without the administration's recommendation, although administrators can, and do, recommend individual teachers for professional assistance.

Staff members and the administration view the program as a benefit for professional growth. Mentors also appreciate the follow-up support. As Sandy Rickenbrode, the district's lead mentor, points out, "As a mentor, it has been wonderful to know that I don't have to try and show my entry-year teacher everything about good teaching in just one year. I know, from experience, that the peer consultants will continue to support and provide the guidance our new colleagues need in order to grow professionally in teaching."

The Plain Local Teachers Association, which is a partner in the program's development, also appreciates the peer consultants' support of professional growth. As President David Ross explains, "Through the five years of the program, teachers welcome the peer consultants as partners in education and perceive them as coaches in the classroom. They are a positive force in the instructional process and in promoting better teaching."

The Evaluation Framework

Unlike mentors, who do not evaluate their novice teachers, peer consultants participate in the district's evaluation framework. Teachers who are new but no longer first-year novices receive professional feedback and evaluation twice a year in both oral and written form. The evaluations from peer consultants—practicing teachers who understand the challenges of classroom instruction—and from administrators, who look for specific indicators of instructional success, offer teachers a more complete picture of their individual progress. To establish a common ground of professional guidelines and language for evaluation, the district has adopted Danielson's (1996) rubrics as a framework for evaluation, self-evaluation, and writing individual professional development plans to meet state guidelines for licensure.

The administrator, peer consultant, and teacher meet for evaluation conferences twice a year, and work together to assess the teacher's individual professional growth. By helping to articulate the teacher's areas of strength and concern, the peer consultants can better help the teachers grow and improve.

The evaluations then go to the Professional Assistance and Review Committee, a group of six members of the teachers association and five administrators that monitors the peer consultant program, approves professional development plans, reviews consultant and administrative evaluations, and recommends further consultant assistance and support as needed. As one of the committee members, Mike Kamionka, notes, the peer consultants play a valuable role: "This program places a great portion of teacher evaluation in the hands of these practicing master teachers. Administrators can then evaluate a teacher in terms of all aspects of the profession and not on the basis of just one or two classroom observations."

Effectiveness of the Program

Although the district believed that the peer consultant program was successful, it wanted to document the program's effectiveness through an in-house evaluation. After reviewing several state programs and determining key points to examine, the district developed a program evaluation tool that used Danielson's (1996) framework elements to evaluate the delivery of assistance by the consultants. It identified 20 elements for review by teacher participants, including number of observations, conferencing availability, and quality of suggestions on classroom management, instructional techniques, and resources. The majority of responses were in the range of good to excellent. The district is using the evaluation's anecdotal suggestions to improve the program (for example, providing additional professional materials) and more time for peer consultants to assist teachers in the classroom.

To evaluate how the program affected teacher retention, the district examined its records for the past five years to determine the number of teacher participants in the peer consultant program who were still employed in Plain Local. Of the 180 teachers who participated, 33 are no longer working in the system. Of those 33 teachers (18 percent), only 3 teachers (1.6 percent) are no longer teaching. Reasons for leaving the district included getting new positions in other districts, moving out of the area, and taking family leave. These statistics are well above the national norm (Recruiting New Teachers, 1999) and confirm the value and effectiveness of the program. As Assistant Superintendent Larry Sullivan points out, "The most important idea behind this program is to help new teachers gain in knowledge, grow in their instruction, and find direction for their future professional growth. The impact on students is apparent through the district's development and retention of strong teachers."

Committed to the continual improvement of teaching, the peer consultant program offers the professional support that new teachers deserve as they begin their careers. It helps fulfill the mission of Plain Local Schools, which is to provide learning experiences for students and collaborative support for new teachers.

References

Danielson, C. (1996). *Enhancing professional practice: A framework for teaching.* Alexandria, VA: Association for Supervision and Curriculum Development.

Educational Testing Service. (2001). *Pathwise orientation guide.* Princeton, NJ: Author.

Evertson, C., & Smithey, M. (1999). *The mentoring handbook: An introduction to mentoring* (4th ed.). Nashville, TN: Vanderbilt Institute.

Galvez-Hjornevik, C. (1986). Teacher mentors: A review of the literature. *Journal of Teacher Education, 37*(1), 6–11.

Recruiting New Teachers. (1999). *Learning the ropes: Urban teacher induction programs and practices in the United States.* Belmont, MA: Author.

Sclan, E. M., & Darling-Hammond, L. (1992). *Beginning teacher performance evaluation: An overview of state policies* (Trends and Issues Paper No. 7). Washington, DC: ERIC Clearinghouse on Teacher Education. American Association of Colleges for Teacher Education.

Sweeny, B. (2000, March). *Mentoring the new teacher.* Presentation at the Association for Supervision and Curriculum Development Annual Conference, New Orleans, LA.

How to Set Up an Induction Program

Susan K. Gardner

Susan K. Gardner taught Spanish for five years at Lincoln High School in Alma Center, Wisconsin, and is currently a doctoral student at Washington State University in Pullman, Washington. She can be reached by e-mail at gardners@wsu.edu.

"Here's the room." These words provided the entire orientation that one teacher received when she began teaching at Lincoln Junior-Senior High School in the Alma Center-Humbird-Merrillan School District in Wisconsin about 10 years ago. The school district for the 1,200 residents of three small towns in this agricultural area had consolidated in 1963, and two schools—one elementary for 340 students and one combined junior and senior high school for 262 students—were located in two different towns and served 93 percent white and 7 percent Mexican American students. Because of the small number of teachers, the low annual turnover rate of staff, and budgetary constraints, the district had not developed an induction program for its new teachers.

Teachers who were new to the district had to rely on their own backgrounds and resources to get through the tumultuous first year of teaching. These teachers usually had the same responsibilities as their more experienced colleagues and were expected to perform and be effective from the first day (Carver, Feiman, Schwille, & Yusko, 1999). As in other small districts, where specialized teachers often constitute the entire department in a particular subject, many teachers felt exceptionally isolated.

Added to these responsibilities and the simple new tasks of finding supplies and staff restrooms, new teachers had to learn how to complete a purchase order, take attendance, complete a budget, and perform many other procedural tasks that most teachers learn only after several years of experience. It is not surprising that many new teachers found themselves overwhelmed, burned out, and exhausted by the second month of school.

Schultz (1999) reports a need for up to 2.5 million new teachers over the next decade, therefore requiring a great need for induction programs in the United States. Unfortunately, as of 2002, only 30 states had teacher-induction programs (Curran & Goldrick, 2002), and one study found that about 22 percent of all new teachers leave within the first three years precisely because of the lack of adequate induction and support (DePaul, 2000).

In 1996, fresh out of college, I began my own teaching career in this small district and experienced the isolation typically felt by new teachers. As I thought about the types of support I needed, I decided to discover how other new teachers felt, and to figure out how our small district could implement an effective induction and mentoring program.

Here are the steps I followed to create and implement an induction and mentoring program for this small district as part of my graduate program in education and professional development. The needs of larger districts may be different, but these are some of the crucial steps.

Get Administrators on Board

First, I approached key administrators—the superintendent and principals of the district's two schools—with my idea. They alerted me to past efforts in this area and suggested resources, such as stipends for mentors, that I had not known about. We agreed that I would spend the first year creating the program and implement it the next year. Investing time to explain my idea in the beginning, and keeping the administrators in the loop throughout the entire process, ensured their strong support.

Conduct Surveys

I developed a survey for teachers and staff members who had been hired within the past five years (see Figure 7.1) and a separate survey for veteran staff members (see Figure 7.2). I also surveyed office secretaries and support staff, who knew firsthand the questions that new and veteran teachers often ask and the problems that they encounter. The survey included general

---

FIGURE 7.1
Staff Survey on Induction Program Development

- Is this your first job working in a school setting after college?

- If not, where did you work before and for how long?

- When you began working in this district, did you feel that you were adequately prepared by the district to begin your job?

- If not, do you believe that having a mentor would have helped?

- Do you believe that this district needs a mentoring program?

- In which areas do you believe that you could have used (or could still use) more information? Circle all that apply:

o Lesson plan/curriculum development	o Preparing for observations
o Layout of the facilities and district	o Contract agreements
o School schedules (daily, monthly)	o Insurance
o General school regulations	o Union issues
o Room arrangements	o Playground and bus duties
o Parent-teacher conferences	o Work order procedures
o Scheduling	o How to order supplies and make purchase orders
o Student assessments	
o Grading policies and report cards	o Inservice days and attendance at conferences
o Roles of other staff members	
o Field trip policies	o Summer school
o Technology resources	o Budgeting
o Copy machines and other office machinery	o Checkout procedures
	o Other (please list)
o Preparing for substitutes	

- Do you believe that an orientation before school started would have helped you?

- Do you believe that monthly or bimonthly sessions discussing some of the items listed above would be helpful for a new employee?

- Please describe any other concerns that you believe should be addressed in an induction program for new employees in our district.

questions about the need for mentoring and induction, and a checklist of procedural and professional assistance that new teachers might want. The response was overwhelming; 80 percent of the staff believed that the school district needed an induction program and circled at least three items on the checklist. The results offered clear evidence of the felt need for an induction and mentoring program and provided the rationale for continuing the project. As the project progressed, I often consulted the survey's comments to guide the development of the program's goals, objectives, and topics for discussion.

Deciding on the focus of the program was important at this juncture. Some induction programs mentor only novice teachers, whereas others choose to include all teachers who are new to the district, new administrators, and even new support staff. Because our district is small and hires only about five new teachers and three support staff each year, we chose to focus on all newcomers to the district.

FIGURE 7.2

Veteran Staff Survey on Induction Program Development

- In what year did you begin teaching in the district?
- What types of support or information did you receive when you began?
- In which areas could you have used more support or information for your first year of teaching?
- Please express your opinion about the development of a mentoring program in our district.

Research Existing Programs

By researching well-established programs, I learned more about what works and what doesn't, and was able to avoid some of the pitfalls that other programs had experienced. I learned, for example, that an induction program should include both a mentoring and an orientation component to have lasting success. The local education service agency had information about other mentoring programs in the area, especially in districts with similar demographics. The Internet, the Educational Resources Information Center (ERIC), and professional books and articles (Baron, Gless, & Moir, 1999; Blair-Larsen, 1998;

Peterson, 1989; Scherer, 1999) provided valuable information about programs throughout the United States and advice on what induction programs should offer. Fawcett (1997), for example, proposes treating teachers as adult learners and arranging induction programs according to different phases of new teacher development.

Present a Proposal

When I presented the results of my survey and research to the administrators, the school board, and the teachers association for their feedback and support, I also proposed the funding and resources that we would need for the project. I requested a yearly stipend for all mentors matched with new teachers, and an additional stipend for those who attended mentor training during the summer. I also suggested adding a day to new teachers' calendars for orientation and initial meetings with mentors.

Members of these groups asked many questions, such as who would serve as a mentor and what the benefits of mentoring would be, and they made recommendations, many of which I was able to include. For example, we realized that sponsoring monthly meetings for mentors and new personnel and providing guides for discussion would be more helpful than sponsoring meetings of only new teachers. These meetings and discussion guides gave the mentors and new teachers more time together and helped maintain a more consistent program.

Because administrators, the school board, and the teachers association were involved in the initial consultations, these groups became strong partners in developing and strengthening the program. The school board's support, for example, became a tangible asset when questions arose about funding the stipends and the additional day of orientation. My suggestion for those who do not receive widespread support from all groups is to suggest running a pilot program for one year and to carefully document its success in terms of the retention of new teachers.

Create a Steering Committee

After receiving approval from all key constituents and appointment as coordinator of the project, I created a steering committee that included a school board member, the superintendent, the principals, and a veteran teacher who had experience in supervising student teachers. As coordinator,

I assigned the committee's duties at the onset, but the committee soon took over defining its role and responsibilities.

We developed a statement of the purpose and mission of the program, and outlined the roles and duties for a mentor, the new staff members, the principals, the coordinator, and other administrators who would be involved in the program. The steering committee chose the mentors, matched them with new teachers, evaluated the program on a regular basis, and made changes as needed.

Recruit Mentors

We created a brochure for potential mentors that described the program's mission statement and goals; what mentors do; the rewards of mentoring, including the district's stipend and the intrinsic benefits of mentoring; the qualifications and responsibilities of a mentor; the training dates; how to obtain an application; and the deadlines for submission and selection. We required mentors to have worked a minimum of three years in the district and to have completed at least some graduate work, preferably a master's degree or coursework in supervising student teachers. The committee then created an application that asked for the applicant's relevant training, special talents, and motivation for becoming a mentor. Because of the small size of the district, we did not need recommendations or interviews.

Before we met to choose mentors, we developed guidelines for selection, including such criteria as assessing each applicant's continuing professional development and demonstrated use of innovative teaching techniques in the classroom. Some districts prefer to develop a pool of mentors from which to choose; others select mentors on the basis of the anticipated needs in the coming school year; and still others look for specific skills and areas of expertise that may be helpful for new teachers. We chose to develop a pool of interested teachers and assign them according to the needs of the new teachers.

Train Mentors

Mentoring is a skill that even the best teachers must learn, so all successful mentoring programs need to include training. The school district may prefer to select an outside expert or develop its own training program. Our district chose to use the two-day sessions offered by state and local education agencies during the summer to train mentors. We also discussed with them our expectations of mentors, such as participating in monthly meetings with their novice teachers, conducting classroom observations at least twice a semester, and serving on the steering committee. Mentors participated in simulations of mentoring situations, learned about effective strategies for observing novices and giving feedback, discussed ways to respond to the needs of new teachers, and made plans for implementing these strategies.

Match Mentors with New Staff

Near the beginning of the next school year, the steering committee met again to match new staff members with mentors. We tried to match those teaching the same grade levels and subject, which was sometimes difficult because of our small size. We had several new special education teachers and teachers with content-area specializations. We found matches of mentors from other specialized fields and used our education service agency to find other specialized teachers in the area. New teachers and mentors had completed interest surveys, which helped the committee choose matches. As a safeguard, we also created an evaluation form that would allow mentors and novices to discontinue their relationship later in the year if the match was not successful.

Orient New Teachers

Our half-day orientation session for new staff members focused only on crucial, need-to-know information about the schools, the district, the community, and, most important, the first week of school. School board members and teachers union representatives joined the group for lunch. In the afternoon, new staff members met one-on-one with their mentors. Traveling in private cars, we gave tours of the school and community, visiting all three townships and focusing on school construction projects, areas from which students traveled by bus to school, and available community resources. To avoid overwhelming new teachers with too much information, we saved sessions on insurances, taxes, and certain kinds of paperwork for later meetings.

I collected all of the forms and procedures for each of the district's schools and created handbooks with alphabetically arranged forms and information. Our secretarial staff provided valuable information about the most commonly asked questions and suggestions about what to include in the handbooks.

Although creating the handbooks was time-consuming, they provided each teacher with a comprehensive resource to refer to as needed. The handbooks were also renewable; we collected the handbooks at the end of the year and updated them for the next year.

Sponsor Monthly Meetings

The steering committee sponsored monthly after-school meetings for new teachers and their mentors. These meetings covered important information that traditional orientations often introduce before school starts and that teachers soon forget. Mentors received discussion guides that included lists of topics to cover, such as upcoming school events, holiday closings, procedures for snow days, budgeting, and contract negotiations. We introduced other topics, such as how to use audiovisual materials, at regular intervals throughout the year.

Many programs use these meetings to help new teachers develop individual goals and to monitor each month's progress with the mentor, but we did not start this process until the second semester, after the new teachers had acclimated to the new environment.

Create Evaluations

Districts can use written evaluations, oral interviews, template evaluations, or rating sheets. Some programs choose to evaluate the program during each monthly session, whereas others may only evaluate twice each semester, as we did.

In addition, we sent evaluation forms every other month to both the mentors and new employees to ask them about their relationship and the program. The committee monitored all evaluations closely and followed up on any problems, changing the program and a few of the pairings when necessary. Especially during the first year of the program, evaluations were extremely helpful in validating the process and documenting the strengths and weaknesses in the program.

Keep Logs and Make Notes

The mentors, new staff members, and steering committee members kept a running log of time spent on different parts of the project and kept notes about frustrations and suggestions for improvements. These logs and notes helped document the requirements for the stipends being earned, indicated how much time commitment was involved in the induction and mentoring process, and kept track of ideas for discussion.

Evaluate Again

At the end of each semester, the steering committee evaluated the program again. It asked the mentors and new employees what they thought about the program, how they felt about the mentoring they had given or received, and what changes would improve the program.

The Profession That Supports Its Young

Some believe that the teaching profession "eats its young," but effective mentoring programs can provide nurturing to support new teachers and help them grow in the profession.

The evaluations and interviews of new staff members in the first end-of-year evaluations indicated that the district's new program was helpful. One new teacher said, "I am extremely pleased with the entire mentoring program. My anxiety about knowing and being responsible for every detail has been immensely alleviated."

The mentors indicated that they enjoyed mentoring and chose to spend a lot more time with their charges than required. They all returned as mentors the following year and are still mentoring. The program has continued and developed since its inception. The quality of the teacher is the single most important factor in improving student achievement in schools (Haycock, 1998). By orienting new teachers to the school, assisting them through the ups and downs of their first year, and helping them become better teachers, effective induction and mentoring programs can foster both teacher retention and student achievement.

References

Baron, W., Gless, J., & Moir, E. (1999). A support program with heart: The Santa Cruz project. In M. Scherer (Ed.), *A better beginning* (pp. 106–115). Alexandria, VA: Association for Supervision and Curriculum Development.

Blair-Larsen, S. (1998). Designing a mentoring program. *Education, 118*(4), 602–605.

Carver, C., Feiman, S., Schwille, S., & Yusko, B. (1999). Beyond support: Taking new teachers seriously as learners. In M. Scherer (Ed.), *A better beginning* (pp. 3–12). Alexandria, VA: Association for Supervision and Curriculum Development.

Curran, B., & Goldrick, L. (2002). *Mentoring and supporting new teachers* (Issue brief). Washington, DC: National Governors Association Center for Best Practices. Available: www.nga.org/cda/files/010902NEWTEACH.pdf

DePaul, A. (2000). *Survival guide for new teachers.* Washington, DC: U.S. Department of Education.

Fawcett, G. (1997). Is a good teacher always a good mentor? *Mentor, 1.* Available: www.mentors.net/for%20Journal1/J1.GTchrGmentor.html

Haycock, K. (1998). Good teaching matters: How well-qualified teachers can close the gap. *Thinking K–16, 3*(2), 1–14. Available: www.edtrust.org/main/documents/k16_summer98.pdf

Peterson, R. (1989, August 8). *Mentor teacher's handbook.* Available: www.gse.uci.edu/MentorTeacher/Preface.html

Scherer, M. (1999). *A better beginning: Supporting and mentoring new teachers.* Alexandria, VA: Association for Supervision and Curriculum Development.

Schultz, B. (1999). Combining mentoring and assessment in California. In M. Scherer (Ed.), *A better beginning* (pp. 99–105). Alexandria, VA: Association for Supervision and Curriculum Development.

Rethinking Induction

Examples from Around the World

Lynn Paine, David Pimm, Edward Britton, Senta Raizen,
and Suzanne Wilson

Lynn Paine (phone: 517-355-3266; e-mail: painel@msu.edu) is an associate professor and David Pimm (phone: 780-492-0753; e-mail: david.pimm@ualberta.ca) and Suzanne Wilson (phone: 517-353-9150; e-mail: swilson@msu.edu) are professors at the College of Education, Michigan State University. Edward Britton (phone: 650-381-6416; e-mail: tbritto@wested.org) and Senta Raizen (phone: 202-467-0652; e-mail: sraizen@wested.org) are associate director and director, respectively, of the National Center for Improving Science Education, WestEd.

Sarah, a first-year science teacher in New Zealand, teaches five classes and sometimes feels overwhelmed by the demands of her new job. But during 20 percent of her day, she has release time for observing other teachers, taking some courses, or just catching up on planning lessons or marking papers. At her school's regular school-based Advice and Guidance meetings for all new teachers, she has the chance to get her deputy principal's suggestions about how to handle time pressures and to discuss many other concerns about life in her classroom and school.

For Bertila, a beginning teacher in Bern, Switzerland, the press of time is also real. She worries that she will "run out of time to do all the things I plan for my lessons—there is so much paperwork to do all the time and the canton's instructional plans really demand a lot." But she has the opportunity to explore these dilemmas with a "practice group" of four other elementary teachers from different schools in Bern. Meeting for eight three-hour sessions, the group members discuss problems and issues in their teaching. Although they work with a trained facilitator, the novice teachers decide the focus for their shared inquiry.

Li Mei, a beginning mathematics teacher in Shanghai, China, has many groups supporting her transition to teaching. To deepen her understanding of the mathematics she teaches, the students she works with, and approaches she can use to help them learn, Li Mei works with a mentor, a group in her school that plans lessons together, a research group that enables her to observe others' teaching, and district-level new-teacher seminar groups. She can't imagine entering the profession without this wide range of guides and opportunities to view and talk about teaching.

Beginning to teach involves both starting a new job and entering a new way of life. New teachers are welcomed and initiated with various degrees of ceremony, and they experience a wide variety of formal or informal procedures intended to help them meet the challenges of this beginning. Whether officially inducted or not, new teachers begin teaching every year, all over the world.

A New Focus on Beginning Teachers

In the United States, this time of transition—from student to teacher, from outsider to insider—is receiving more attention than ever before. Increasingly, states, districts, and national organizations are recognizing the importance of the teacher's early career. Thirty-three states now have policies on induction, compared with only 15 in the 1980s (American Federation of Teachers, 2001). Many national organizations have also begun to target induction. Both the National Council for Accreditation of Teacher Education and the American Association of Colleges for Teacher Education have urged teacher preparation programs to begin actively following up with their graduates. The National Research Council (2001) included significant attention to teacher induction in its sweeping recommendations for reforms in teacher preparation.

Why the attention? Teacher retention has become a serious concern in the United States. Approximately one-third of beginning teachers leave teaching within the first five years, and the attrition rates are even higher in urban schools and high-poverty schools (Darling-Hammond, 2003). Schools are scrambling to hire and retain teachers, especially in science and mathematics. Teacher retirements, growing enrollments, and class-size reduction policies have added to the increased demand for teachers. Induction offers a way not only to keep new teachers in the profession, but also to help them consolidate their craft and move beyond an initial focus on classroom management issues (National Commission on Teaching and America's Future, 1996).

Most discussions about induction, and most programs in place today in the United States, focus on providing psychological and moral support for new teachers—usually by connecting the novice with a mentor—or creating mechanisms for early assessment (Feiman-Nemser, Carver, Schwille, & Yusko, 1999; Gold, 1996). To help attract teachers to a learning profession and to provide ways of keeping teachers engaged in that profession, induction must go beyond support and do more than assess teachers.

A different and more promising approach treats induction as a distinct phase in a teacher's learning career. The first few years on the job create opportunities for teachers to gain knowledge and understandings that they could not learn in their teacher preparation programs (Feiman-Nemser, 2003). Good induction programs create the conditions for developing the vital skills that can be learned only from practice.

How can we reimagine induction as an opportunity for this kind of learning? How can we understand it as more than simply filling in gaps or providing moral support for the novice teacher? Like fish in a fish tank, we may not recognize the water in which we swim. By looking beyond our national borders and considering the experiences of induction in different parts of the world, we can consider a broader range of possibilities and challenge our assumptions about what new teachers need and how schools can help them grow.

Studying Induction in Four Countries

From 1998–2002, we were involved in a study funded by the National Science Foundation that focused on induction for middle-grade mathematics and science teachers in selected countries (Britton, Paine, Pimm, & Raizen, 2003). After an initial exploratory phase that studied induction in 12 countries, we selected four countries in which to do more intensive fieldwork. In France, China (Shanghai), New Zealand, and Switzerland, we conducted one to three months of interviews and observations to examine induction policies, programs, and practices.

The study attempted to capture, in each national context, both the range of settings in which induction activities took place and the important features of the national education landscape. To accomplish this, we adapted the case study design for each site. (See Figure 8.1 for a list of dominant activities in each country.)

France. Although nationally articulated, French induction policy plays out primarily through regional institutions and schools in each Academy (the regional organizational structure responsible for all K–12, induction, and inservice education). Our work focused on the experiences of teachers in two Academies in Paris. We also examined practices in the higher education institutions, called IUFM (University Institutes for the Formation of Teachers), which are responsible for induction programs and continuing teacher education. In addition, we studied teaching and mentoring in 10 schools and conducted interviews with policymakers, inspectors, mathematics educators, and mathematics education researchers.

China. Shanghai's approach to induction, mandated at the municipal level, is funded by districts, schools and—in some cases—teachers themselves. We interviewed central administrators and conducted intensive data collection in four districts that reflect a range of economic, demographic, and education contexts. We interviewed district staff developers and teacher educators in each district, as well as teachers and administrators in 21 schools. We also conducted less detailed interviews and surveys of teachers in other districts.

New Zealand. There is no intermediate level between the national government and schools in New Zealand. Its national policy of induction, although centrally funded, is largely school-based. We therefore focused data collection on schools, observing and interviewing teachers and administrators in 15 schools in the two major cities, Auckland and Wellington.

Switzerland. The Swiss education system and its approaches to induction are highly decentralized. Cantons—the equivalent of states, each with their own education ministry—pay for facilities, permanent central staff, and mentors and counselors. The cantons also subsidize new teachers for their participation in induction activities by providing substitute teachers. We focused our work in three cantons: Bern, Lucerne, and Zurich. There we observed and conducted interviews in schools, practice groups, and teacher education programs.

These four countries reflect great variation in their level of centralization, organization of the teaching force, education philosophies, and the reforms in play. Yet as we look across the sites, we note a surprising pattern of similarity. All of these education systems employ comprehensive teacher induction—both in terms of the purposes of induction and in terms of the strategies used to promote new teacher learning (Britton, Paine, Pimm, & Raizen, 2003).

What New Teachers Need to Learn

We have noted that the most common goal of new teacher induction programs in the United States is providing personal support for new teachers to help them adjust to the classroom and survive their first few years. In contrast, the four countries that we studied exhibit broad cross-national agreement that the novice teacher's central task—a complex, demanding, and time-consuming one—is learning to teach. Even in Switzerland, where extensive preservice teacher preparation provides a solid grounding in both subject specialization and pedagogy, schools assume that every beginning teacher needs opportunities to learn.

What do schools in these settings identify as the skills that teachers need to learn? The induction goals in all four countries stress the importance of

- Effective subject-matter teaching.
- Understanding and meeting pupils' needs.
- Assessing pupil work and learning.
- Engaging in reflective and inquiry-oriented practice.
- Dealing with parents.
- Understanding school organization and participating in the school community.
- Understanding oneself and the current status of one's career.

This list forcefully reminds us of the demanding nature of teaching as a practice. Clearly, nobody can fully master these matters in advance of taking on responsibility as a classroom teacher. But novice teachers must gain competence in these skills early in their careers.

The programs that we studied reflect remarkable agreement in focusing on both improving teaching quality and enhancing personal development. In addition to offering emotional and psychological support to the new teacher, induction programs in these settings make it possible for novice teachers to take the knowledge that they learned in preservice preparation and deepen it. These programs also create occasions in which teachers can learn knowledge and skills that they had no opportunity to develop prior to teaching. Going beyond support or orientation, these programs treat teachers not just as beginners, but also as learners.

In addition, all of these sites include attention to subject-specific aspects of teacher induction. U.S. induction programs rarely give explicit attention to subject-specific needs. In contrast, beginning mathematics teachers in France—despite having already studied three or more years of university mathematics—spend one day each week at the University Institute for the Formation of Teachers working on developing the pedagogical content knowledge of mathematics. At the end of their first year of teaching, they must defend before a jury a yearlong project on some aspect of teaching mathematics. In this *professional memoir*, they study a mathematics teaching issue arising in and from their practice, connected to the field of mathematics education research and contributing to it.

Practices to Support New Teachers' Learning

What activities do schools in these five countries use to support the goals of induction? Figure 8.1 outlines the major activities in each site. For the most part, the activities are closely connected to practice. As we examine the range of induction activities across the settings, certain patterns stand out.

Diverse Activities Within Programs

In each of these settings, induction involves a wide range of activities. Programs are developed with the assumption that beginning teachers need different approaches and formats to support the broad range of learning and development required of them.

In New Zealand, for example, induction involves both school-based Advice and Guidance discussions and out-of-school seminars. The former involves regular (often biweekly) meetings of all the beginning teachers in a school. Wide-ranging discussions deal with personal and professional concerns. For example, teachers discuss the first week of school, classroom management, sports, the history of the school, and cultural differences. Out-of-school opportunities

---

FIGURE 8.1
Dominant Induction Activities in Four Countries

France

- Work with mentor or pedagogic advisor in own school
- Assist an experienced teacher in another school (*accompanied practice*)
- Take courses at the University Institute for the Formation of Teachers one day each week in subject-area groups and half a day in general pedagogical issues
- Conduct a yearlong research project (*professional memoir*) assisted by a memoir mentor

New Zealand

- Work with a supervisor
- Be observed and observe others
- Work with a buddy teacher
- Attend advice and guidance group meetings
- Have release time/free periods
- Outside of school: attend new-teacher workshops

China (Shanghai)

- Work with mentors—specifically, a subject-specific mentor who supports instructional work, and a class director mentor who supports learning how to serve as a *banzhuren,* or director for a homeroom or class of students
- Observe others' teaching and participate in debriefing discussions that follow—within one's own school and at other schools
- Prepare a report lesson (an open lesson given by the novice)
- Participate in teaching competitions
- Attend district workshops and seminars for new teachers

Switzerland

- Participate in practice groups
- Participate in classroom observation
- Develop a *Standortbestimmung* (a self-evaluation and reflection), usually with help from a counselor or mentor
- Receive individual or group counseling, often about the daily life and work of teaching

---

FIGURE 8.1 (*continued*)

Dominant Induction Activities in Four Countries

- Attend courses and professional development classes—in Zurich, a four-week summer course; in all cantons in the study, short-term and needs-based seminars and courses

- Receive mentoring (dominant in Lucerne; available but not a prominent part of induction in Bern and Zurich)

Note: *Although patterns vary within each country, these represent the major components of induction activity that are part of most novices' experience. In Switzerland, differences between canton induction programs complicate the portrait, as does the fact that novices tend to choose from a menu of options instead of feeling obligated to participate in everything.*

---

include subject-specific workshops organized by regional Advisory Services, follow-up workshops conducted by teacher preparation programs for their graduates, and university courses designed for beginning teachers.

In France, the first-year teacher teaches only part-time in one school, while assisting an experienced teacher in a second school (an activity called an *accompanied practice*) and taking courses each week at the IUFM, the higher education institution designed to support teacher learning.

The range of options for novice teachers in Switzerland includes practice groups, such as the one that Bertila attends; observation of other teachers; seminars and courses; and individual counseling for any new teacher who wants it. In addition, each beginning teacher undertakes, usually with the help of a mentor, a reflective activity called a *Standortbestimmung* ("a determination of status") to examine where he or she stands as a teacher and as a person. This process is a self-evaluation of self-competence, social competence, and competence in one's area of teaching. It leads to a determination of next steps in self- and professional development.

Li Mei and other beginners in Shanghai participate in a range of required and voluntary activities, both in and out of school, that includes demonstration lessons, school-level and district-level mentoring, teaching competitions, school orientations, district seminars, subject-specific hot-lines, and more.

Learning Tied to Practice

Induction provides opportunities for novices to look closely at teaching through specific activities and relationships. In the programs we studied, new teachers observe and are observed; discuss individual lessons with their mentors and sometimes with others; and are encouraged to talk about particular pupils. We found at least three kinds of activities that were common across the sites: mentoring, peer-group activity, and reflective work.

Working closely with a mentor. In every site, beginning teachers have the opportunity (in most cases, the requirement) to work one-on-one with an experienced teacher. We found it intriguing that the terms used to describe this role vary by site and that different connotations were associated with these terms.

The words used in Shanghai have a strong colloquial feel to them—*guiding teacher*, *old teacher*, or *master* (and they imply a counterpart—one being led, a *disciple* or a *new teacher*). All Shanghai beginners work with two different kinds of mentors. The subject-specific mentor supports the novice's instructional work through collaborative planning, observations, and post-observation debriefings. Another mentor helps a beginner learn to take on the diverse duties of a "class director." The novice shadows this mentor, who convenes a cohort of students and is responsible for supporting each child's social, personal, and academic development throughout the year.

France has its *pedagogic advisors*, a title that accurately suggests that their work focuses on instructional expertise. In contrast, New Zealand's *Advice and Guidance advisors*, *department heads*, and *buddy teachers* together might be seen as taking on different mentor-like roles. The Advice and Guidance advisor, usually the school's deputy principal, creates the Advice and Guidance program for the first-year and second-year teachers, including convening and running the regular Advice and Guidance meetings for all these teachers. This advisor also looks out for the novices' personal welfare, as a sort of "mother hen," as one advisor explained. Department chairs observe beginners' classes both formally and informally, hold one-on-one meetings with them, invite beginners to observe their classes, and alert them to professional development opportunities outside the school. Buddy teachers are assigned as another resource, a teacher often chosen to complement the skills and attributes of the department head. Sometimes the teacher next door, and often closer in age to the novice, the buddy teacher can offer quick help and support on an impromptu basis.

In Switzerland, mentoring is the main form of induction in upper secondary school. It is one-on-one, sometimes provided by the same teacher who supervised the student teaching practicum of the beginning teacher. The mentor may observe as often as once a week and hold discussions with the new teacher afterward.

Despite the linguistic variation, mentor programs share the underlying assumption that one does not become a teacher alone or in isolation. Experience helps, and the novice can tap into the collective experience of the profession through close, sustained contact with a more experienced teacher.

Connecting with peers. Many U.S. programs mandate that novice teachers work with mentors, but the interactions among novices that we observed in the international sites is less prevalent in the United States. In each of the settings we studied, induction providers created regular opportunities for novices to share, discuss, plan, investigate, support, and vent with other beginners. Induction can help beginners develop collegial relationships with their peers. The new teachers whom we interviewed clearly valued the trading and sharing of experiences with others who faced some of the same challenges of transition. As Sarah explained after participating in a workshop with other first-year teachers, "Everyone felt overwhelmed by the job. I was so relieved to know that I wasn't the only one who had been discouraged by classroom management problems."

Peer observation, peer reflection, and joint inquiry projects all reinforce the idea that novices can learn from one another. Switzerland's practice groups offer perhaps the clearest example of the attention and value given to such connections. First-year and second-year teachers from different schools can voluntarily form a group to discuss problems on a regular basis. Meeting six to eight times during the year for about three hours each session, the participants try to resolve problems in their practices, drawing on shared observations of one another's teaching to anchor the discussions. The novices themselves direct the group discussions, but each group has a well-trained, carefully selected facilitator.

Reflecting, inquiring, and researching. Induction can also push beginners to look closely at their own practice by creating activities that focus on reflection and inquiry. Through these, beginning teachers develop a reflective stance, personally and professionally.

The *Standortbestimmung* reflective activity in Switzerland exemplifies the importance that Swiss educators place on the personal aspect of teacher development. A reflection on one's professional growth, it takes place either in the context of personal counseling (available to the novices as one option in induction and usually by the practice group leader) or as a culminating experience during the last meeting of a practice group. The beginner engages in a self-evaluation and contemplates future personal and professional development.

The professional memoir typifies France's interest in having new teachers develop analytical and reflective skills that they can bring to bear on aspects of their own emerging practice, including—in the case of mathematics—task design and the use of curriculum materials and pedagogic resources.

Learning Outside the Novice's Classroom

Schools in the countries studied act on the belief that new teachers' learning can be amplified by activities outside of their own classroom. Thus, each system also provides opportunities for beginners to participate in activities out of school: courses at the University Institute for the Formation of Teachers and regular visits to another teacher's classroom through accompanied practice in France, occasional seminars in New Zealand, and practice groups in Switzerland. In Japan, a teacher cruise ship takes about 20 percent of the nation's new teachers on a summer cruise each year that emphasizes cultural activities. These induction activities all rest on the belief that beginners need some distance from the immediacy of the classroom in order to see their teaching in new ways.

Sufficient Time for Learning

Induction takes time. The experience in all of these sites suggests that it takes time and effort to make the necessary arrangements, establish relationships, link the beginning teacher to effective instructional practices and curriculum, and more.

Notice, for example, the frequency and intensity of induction activities in these programs. The total number of hours is impressive:

- Shanghai beginners undertake a minimum of 100 hours of induction activity, although we consistently observed novices engaged in even more hours of intensive induction.
- French first-year mathematics teachers have their entire week arranged to support induction: attending classes for a day and a half at the University Institute for the Formation of Teachers; teaching a single class by themselves in one school throughout the entire year; developing and presenting a professional memoir; and supporting and observing an experienced teacher at another school, usually for a block of 12 weeks during the year.
- In New Zealand, weekly Advice and Guidance meetings, coupled with a range of other activities, constitute 20 percent of the beginning teacher's schedule.
- The Swiss cantons we studied had no uniform time requirement, yet in each setting induction activities were intensive. Practice groups in Lucerne meet for 30 hours in the course of the beginner's first year, and each novice also spends 20 hours on classroom observation. Zurich's program requires two years from beginning teachers. Toward the end of the first year, they must take an intensive four-week course. They are also entitled to individual counseling and may request up to 32 hours of counseling during their induction period.

Just as important, each induction activity in these four locations is sustained over time. Working with a mentor, constructing a professional memoir, and participating in a practice group all involve repeated interactions over a substantial period, giving novice teachers the opportunity to develop relationships, dig into a topic, consider alternative views, and gather and explore data.

Reflecting on Substantive Education Issues

The induction system in each of these countries encourages beginning teachers to think deeply, often collectively, about specific aspects of teaching. Novices engage with difficult issues that they face in their own classrooms: the challenges of planning, the design of learning tasks, the management of education settings for learning, the dilemmas of assessment, and so on. Induction creates opportunities for teachers early in their careers to work in targeted ways on broadly conceived elements of their own practice. The focus of the activities demonstrates the complexity of teaching, whether that focus is on subject-matter instruction, as in France, or more wide-ranging issues, as in New Zealand.

Two practices in Shanghai—report lessons and the teaching competition—provide opportunities to deepen new teachers' understandings of the many dimensions of teaching. Shanghai beginning teachers conduct at least one report lesson as part of their induction. The beginner teaches a class that is observed by colleagues and sometimes outsiders. Following the class, the novice offers a reflection on the lesson and engages in a discussion with the observers.

In the teaching competition sponsored by the city and its districts, new teachers develop and explain a lesson plan, working closely with colleagues as they develop their ideas. Schools, districts, and the municipal authorities hold competitions each year, and schools may expect their new teachers to participate at least once in their induction period. Typically working as a tiered system, the competitions have winners from the lower level go on to compete at the next. At each level, panels composed of expert teachers and local professional development specialists judge the candidates. Although winners receive a small monetary reward, the real prize is the honor and distinction.

In both the report lessons and the teaching competitions, beginning teachers must reflect on the ways in which content and learners come together so that they can articulate and argue for the benefits of their pedagogical decisions before a panel of expert teachers. The intense preparation for these events, as well as the lively conversations that follow them, reinforce new teachers' recognition that teaching is an intellectually demanding practice that requires advanced knowledge, skill, and judgment.

In these sites, induction typically focuses less on sharing techniques than on encouraging problem solving as a necessary skill for teachers. Not surprisingly, the induction programs that we observed—for example, the Swiss practice group with its wide-ranging conversations, reflections, and guided discussions—were complex, both in the individual activities and in their combination.

Rethinking the Purposes of Induction

Looking at these international examples, we see that induction programs vary tremendously in their particular arrangements but share remarkably similar goals. The heart of induction in all of these sites is an effort to make the transition to teaching a period of intense and productive teacher learning. Although teacher recruitment was a motivating factor in establishing the current induction approach in France, and teacher retention is still an ongoing problem in Shanghai and Switzerland, schools in all of these sites value induction for more than its ability to respond to problems of teacher hiring or retention. They view the induction period as an essential tool that supports the learning and growth of new teachers.

In these sites, the purpose of induction is not primarily to fix problems, but to build something desirable: effective teachers, a strong teaching force, a vital profession, and optimum learning for students in schools. When we commented in a Shanghai interview on the many efforts directed toward assisting new teachers there, a young teacher corrected us, "It's not for the teachers; it's for the pupils." She was right. If we rethink induction and recognize that it can encompass not only teacher support and assessment but also teacher learning, we can use this special period in the professional lives of teachers to accomplish much broader goals.

References

American Federation of Teachers. (2001). Beginning teacher induction: The essential bridge. *Educational Policy Briefs* (No. 13). Washington, DC: AFT Educational Issues Department.

Britton, E., Paine, L., Pimm, D., & Raizen, S. (2003). *Comprehensive teacher induction: Systems for early career learning.* Dordrecht, Holland: Kluwer Academic Publishers.

Darling-Hammond, L. (2003). Keeping good teachers: Why it matters, what leaders can do. *Educational Leadership, 60*(8), 6–13.

Feiman-Nemsar, S. (2003). What new teachers need to learn. *Educational Leadership, 60*(8), 25–29.

Feiman-Nemser, S., Carver, C., Schwille, S., & Yusko, B. (1999). Beyond support: Taking new teachers seriously as learners. In M. Scherer (Ed.), *A better beginning: Supporting and mentoring new teachers* (pp. 3–12). Alexandria, VA: Association for Supervision and Curriculum Development.

Gold, Y. (1996). Beginning teacher support: Attrition, mentoring, and induction. In J. Sikula (Ed.), *Handbook of research on teacher education* (pp. 548–594). New York: Macmillan.

National Commission on Teaching and America's Future. (1996). *What matters most: Teaching for America's future.* New York: Author.

National Research Council. (2001). *Educating Teachers of Science, Mathematics, and Technology.* Washington, DC: Author.

Renewing Urban Teachers Through Mentoring

Felicia Saffold

Felicia Saffold is an assistant professor in the Department of Curriculum and Instruction, School of Education, University of Wisconsin-Milwaukee, Enderis Hall, P.O. Box 413, Milwaukee, WI 53201. She can also be reached by e-mail at fsaffold@uwm.edu.

Policymakers are increasingly concerned about recruiting and retaining a strong teaching force, especially reducing the high attrition rates among new teachers. To meet the demands of expanding student enrollments, class size reductions, and accelerating retirement rates, U.S. schools will need to hire more than 2 million new teachers during the next decade (Archer, 1999; Darling-Hammond, 1997). The loss of new teachers is particularly acute in urban school districts, where teacher turnover is as high as 50 percent in the first three years of teaching (Haberman & Rickards, 1990; Odell, 1990).

To address these problems and develop a more diverse teaching force, Milwaukee set up the Dorothy Danforth Compton Fellowship Program in 1996 to recruit, prepare, and retain new middle school teachers of color. A collaborative effort among the Milwaukee Public Schools, Marquette University, Alverno College, and Lakeland College, the alternative licensure program offers high-quality teacher preparation to approximately 50 individuals each year who have completed bachelor's degrees from accredited institutions but have not completed a certification program. Most are midcareer changers.

At the end of the year's program, after 16 graduate credit hours that include student teaching, each Fellow defends a portfolio that demonstrates competency in the performance-based standards established by the

Wisconsin Standards for Teacher Development and Licensure (see www.dpi.state.wi.us/dpi/dlsis/tel/stand10.html) and the Interstate New Teacher Assessment and Support Consortium (INTASC) (see www.ccsso.org/intasc .html). On successful completion of the one-year program, teachers are guaranteed a contract in the Milwaukee Public Schools and recommended for grade 5–8 certification by one of the three participating colleges. To date, the program has produced 174 new teachers of color who now teach in Milwaukee's schools.

The Role of Mentors

Each participant works with a supervisor and the faculty members of their required graduate courses, but each Fellow's most crucial relationship is with a mentor, a veteran teacher who works full time as a coach to approximately seven Fellows. Mentors offer ideas, model instructional strategies, team teach, collaborate on lesson planning, supply resources, and engage in ongoing problem solving with their assigned Fellows. Because the program is grounded in the INTASC standards, the full-time mentors can help Compton Fellows meet the performance assessment standards that are incorporated in the Milwaukee Public Schools curriculum. Through daily on-the-job coaching, mentors help the Compton Fellows learn the INTASC standards and pedagogy.

Milwaukee recruits mentors from a pool of those who have taught for at least five years, demonstrated successful urban teaching practices, received strong recommendations from school principals or administrators, and had some experience teaching adults. In particular, mentors must have demonstrated the characteristics of "star teachers" of urban students: high expectations for all students, persistence, love of learning, and the ability to convince students that learning is good, natural, and enjoyable (Haberman, 1995). Mentors receive training in cognitive coaching and interactive skills. As instructional leaders and successful urban veteran teachers, the mentors provide professional lifelines to the Compton Fellows.

Mentors are able to help Fellows try new strategies that reach beyond the traditional textbook curriculum. In one case, a Fellow complained that his students wouldn't write in class. The mentor suggested that he encourage students to write about a topic of personal interest. The Fellow had the students write letters to the local television station about its cancellation of a popular television show. The students had plenty to say, and the new teacher was able to teach them how to write a business letter.

Benefits for Mentors

Mentors clearly help support and retain new teachers, but the mentoring experience also helps refresh and retain veteran teachers. Those who step out of their classrooms for this three-year coaching position increase their knowledge of the performance-based standards and strengthen their teaching and leadership skills. During my interviews with Compton Fellowship Program mentors (Edwards, 2001), they described four specific benefits of participating in the program: improved reflective practices, a higher level of professional responsibility, a broadened view of the profession, and a renewed appreciation for the field of education.

Improved Reflective Practices

Most teacher educators consider journal writing as synonymous with reflective practice, and research suggests that journal writing facilitates the analysis of learning and putting learning into practice (Schon, 1983, 1987). Mentoring, however, provides a context for substantive reflective practices that go beyond journal writing. One mentor explained, "Because I had to answer so many questions asked by the Fellows, I had to reexamine my teaching practices. I had never thought about why I present material as I do, such as incorporating the daily newspaper into many subjects and developing learning centers to keep students excited about the subject."

Through the mentoring experience, mentors began to value how much they had learned over the years. As one mentor stated:

> I have developed quite a big bag of tricks over the years. I guess I really never thought about it, but when I walk into a teacher's room and see the problems that he or she is having, I remember why I came up with some of my strategies.
>
> For example, at the start of each class, I always have a brain teaser or riddle on the board. As my students walk in to the room, they know that they have about five minutes to solve the day's challenge. This strategy motivates students to come to class on time and focus on the challenge. And it gives them something constructive to do while I take attendance. The daily challenge cuts down on a lot of behavior problems. When I share strategies like these, I realize how far I have come.

Reflection benefited both mentors and Fellows. Articulating classroom practices helped mentors develop as educators and helped Fellows learn how to evaluate their own work. One mentor commented, "In the beginning, my Fellows all wanted me to tell them what they were doing wrong, but now most of them are able to identify their own strengths and weaknesses."

Higher Level of Professional Activity

Mentors had many opportunities to engage in professional discourse and to share their expertise with peers in the program and with other teachers. One mentor, for example, commenting on the professional development sessions she had held at her assigned school, said, "I love being able to hold workshops after school. First, I was just working with my group of seven Fellows, but then the principal asked me to work with other teachers. I have a lot of experience in exceptional education, and I love teaching adults about effective ways to work with exceptional education students."

Another mentor reported that she enjoyed being able to make a professional presentation at a conference: "I never would have thought that I could do anything like this before becoming a mentor. My confidence has just shot up."

Their new responsibilities also offered mentors more opportunities to expand their knowledge of education by reading professional journals and keeping up with current issues in education. One mentor said, "I read a lot, and I share articles with my Fellows. I am able to contribute to their knowledge base, and I know so much more about teaching and learning than I did before."

Educators often underestimate the value of professional discourse in the development of teachers, but one of the most powerful approaches to developing confidence about teaching practices is ongoing professional conversation among colleagues (Routman, 2002). The Compton mentors met biweekly for team meetings to discuss their responsibilities. These meetings and the professional materials that they read on their own and together—such as *The First Days of School* (Wong & Wong, 2001) and *Other People's Children* (Delpit, 1995)—gave the mentors practical ideas and increased their confidence. One commented, "It is great being able to sit down and have conversations about education with my colleagues. The only time I ever had the opportunity to really do this was when I was taking graduate courses. This professional dialogue is one of the highlights of being a mentor."

Broader View of the Profession

Teachers need experiences beyond their own school building and classroom, and full-time mentoring offers such opportunities: "I never really knew anything about what anyone else was teaching or what other schools were like. This experience has opened my eyes."

Several mentors stated that they had a much broader sense of the quality of education throughout the district. For example, one mentor noted, "I never knew that so many of the subject areas are using performance assessments to evaluate student performance."

Mentors were often surprised to find out that exceptional practices were taking place in schools all across the district. One mentor said, "I thought my school was the only place where I would want to work, but now I have changed my tune. There are quite a few schools I would consider going to."

Mentors also bring new perspectives to the different schools in which they work. Mentors can nurture new teachers' growth and confidence, and they can keep new teachers from developing the negative attitudes that novices often adopt about teaching in urban districts and about coping with the schools' bureaucratic demands.

Renewed Commitment to Education

Before they began mentoring, several mentors were contemplating leaving the field of education. By seeing teaching through fresh eyes, mentors were able to remember why they went into teaching in the first place. One mentor commented that she hadn't felt respected or appreciated as a teacher after seven years of teaching in the system, but becoming a mentor changed that. She said, "Helping the Fellows make sense of what it means to be a teacher reminds me why I went into the field in the first place. Mentoring has renewed my enthusiasm for the teaching profession."

Some mentors spoke of how the experience fueled their ambition to take on administrative roles in education. Although none of the mentors reported being dissatisfied with mentoring, several stated that it was not as fulfilling as being in the classroom. One mentor described the renewal process best when she said:

Being out of the classroom is a good experience for a short time. You learn a great deal and you contribute to the growth of a beginner. All veteran teachers should have this experience. But I can't wait to get back to my elementary classroom. Mentoring was a wonderful experience for me. Now I know, without a shadow of a doubt, that I need to teach!

Success

Of the 195 new teachers who completed the program, 94 percent remained in the Milwaukee Public Schools, and 75 percent of those reported that having a mentor during their first year influenced their decision to stay in teaching (Edwards, 2002). The Compton Fellowship Program has proven to be a success for the Milwaukee Public Schools, the Compton Fellows, and the mentors who coached them. The program began with the vision of recruiting, preparing, and supporting new teachers. That vision remains constant, yet we have also discovered that the program clearly provides new ways for veteran urban teachers to refine their practices, take on leadership roles, and make valuable contributions to the profession.

Mentoring programs are crucial for retaining urban teachers. Those who design such programs should carefully consider how veteran teachers can receive mentoring's full benefits. Then, perhaps, more veteran teachers will experience a renewed commitment to the profession.

References

Archer, J. (1999). Teacher recruitment group branches out, asserts itself. *Education Week, 18*(36), 6–7.

Darling-Hammond, L. (1997). *Doing what matters most: Investing in quality teaching.* New York: National Commission on Teaching and America's Future.

Delpit, L. (1995). *Other people's children: Cultural conflict in the classroom.* New York: The New Press.

Edwards, F. (2001). *Benefits of being a mentor.* Unpublished manuscript, Cardinal Stritch University, Milwaukee, Wisconsin.

Edwards, F. (2002). *The impact of mentoring on new teacher retention: Perceptions of urban schoolteachers.* Unpublished doctoral dissertation, Cardinal Stritch University, Milwaukee, Wisconsin.

Haberman, M. (1995). *Star teachers of children in poverty.* Bloomington, IN: Kappa Delta Pi.

Haberman, M., & Rickards, W. R. (1990). Urban teachers who quit: Why they leave and what they do. *Urban Education, 25*(3), 297–303.

Odell, S. J. (1990). Support for new teachers in mentoring. In T. M. Bey & C. T. Holmes (Eds.), *Mentoring: Developing successful new teachers* (pp. 3–23). Reston, VA: Association of Teacher Educators.

Routman, R. (2002). Teacher talk. *Educational Leadership, 59*(6) 32–35.

Schon, D. A. (1983). *The reflective practitioner*. New York: BasicBooks.

Schon, D. A. (1987). *Educating the reflective practitioner: Toward a new design for teaching and learning in the professions*. San Francisco: Jossey-Bass.

Wong, H. K., & Wong, R. T. (2001). *The first days of school* (2nd ed.). Mountain View, CA: Harry K. Wong Publications.

Part III

Valuing Good Teachers

10

Giving True Value

A Model for Teacher Compensation

Christopher R. Gareis, James H. Stronge,
and Catherine A. Little

Christopher R. Gareis is Associate Dean for Professional Services, School of Education, The College of William and Mary; he can be reached by phone at (757) 221-2319 or by e-mail at crgare@wm.edu. James H. Stronge is Heritage Professor of Education in Educational Planning, Policy, and Leadership, The College of William and Mary; he can be reached by phone at (757) 221-2339 or by e-mail at jhstro@wm.edu. Catherine A. Little is Curriculum and Program Development Coordinator, Center for Gifted Education, The College of William and Mary; she can be reached by phone at (757) 221-2588 or by e-mail at calitt@wm.edu.

Before the first bell rings in a new school year, an average of three out of every 10 prospective new teachers have decided not to enter the profession for which they have prepared (Edwards, 2000). Of the remaining seven, at least one will not return after his or her first year in the classroom. By the end of the third year—the year during which most school districts grant tenure to satisfactory teachers—at least one more from this cohort will have departed (Ingersoll, 2002). Of the original 10 teachers, only five will remain by the end of the fourth year. A .500 average is fantastic for baseball. In teaching, it's nothing short of a crisis.

The attrition continues throughout the ensuing years of teaching. One national study concluded that 90 percent of new hires in a typical school district are replacements for teachers who have left the district. No doubt some of these departing teachers have retired, and others have moved to different school districts for personal reasons. But most new hires replace veteran teachers who left the classroom because of dissatisfaction related to a lack of administrator support, a lack of autonomy in their teaching, and low pay (Ingersoll, 2002).

The crisis has reached such proportions that even the general public is alarmed. In Phi Delta Kappa's annual Gallup poll, respondents identified "getting good teachers" as the second most serious problem facing public schools, trailing only student discipline (Rose & Gallup, 2002). The federal government also identified the teaching shortage as a major problem. The No Child Left Behind Act passed by Congress in 2002 mandates that every child in the United States be taught by a "highly qualified teacher" by the year 2005–2006. Some policymakers propose that states meet this goal by changing licensing requirements to open up alternate routes to teaching. But this strategy misses the point: The teacher shortage is not simply an issue of attracting qualified people to the profession; the real challenge is keeping them there. One 47-year-old veteran teacher wrote in an online forum:

> This is looking like a dead-end job. I have excellent credentials, a good record of student achievement, state awards, national awards, a master's degree, National Board certification, a flawless attendance record, excellent reviews, an adjunct position at a local university, a chair on the board of a state-sponsored professional development program. Yet, I am not convinced that anyone wants to keep someone like me.

Federal legislation calling for a highly qualified teacher in every classroom will prove hollow unless midcareer professionals come to feel that school districts value their work and accomplishments.

Although few teachers report that they entered the profession for the money, many who leave cite the low pay as a major reason for their dissatisfaction (Ingersoll, 2002). Compensation does play a major role in retaining teachers. But the issue is not just *how much* we pay teachers. Indeed, with more than half of the states declaring major budgetary crises in the midst of a floundering national economy, the public coffers probably could not support any significant across-the-board increase in teacher compensation. Instead, we need to ask: How can we structure teacher compensation packages to demonstrate that we value teachers' work?

The Traditional Salary Schedule

Today, most school districts in the United States compensate teachers on the basis of a uniform salary schedule that reflects their years of service and their attainment of advanced degrees. This system, which has been in place for nearly a century, has much to commend it. Most educators view the traditional salary schedule as fair, free of the potential biases or whims of administrators, easy to understand, and easy to administer.

Two key assumptions underlie this system: that the greater the teacher's experience and education level, the better he or she performs; and that basing teacher compensation on these measures will motivate teachers throughout their career. Increasingly, however, critics of traditional compensation systems question these assumptions. These critics contend that the system simply rewards teachers for putting in time, offers no incentive for exemplary performance, and does little to improve poor performance—key issues in a time of increasing public scrutiny, high-stakes testing, and teacher shortages.

One School District's Experience

Our focus on teacher pay grew out of our longstanding concern with teacher supervision and evaluation and, more specifically, our work in developing multidata teacher evaluation systems that are based on defined teacher competencies (Stronge & Tucker, 2002). We collaborated with a school district located in a diverse major metropolitan area that employs approximately 1,300 teachers. The district leaders asked us to help them create a locally responsive teacher performance evaluation system to promote measurable indicators of goal attainment. As that work progressed, a growing recognition of the inextricable links between evaluation and compensation emerged among the district's school board and key leaders. At the request of the school board, and with the partnership of a representative committee of teachers and administrators, we turned our attention to the issue of performance-based pay.

The district's salary schedule had been in place longer than anyone could remember and had been adjusted many times over the years to respond to changes in teacher demographics and economic fluctuations. In recent years, however, school board members and teachers began raising concerns that the salary schedule did not meet the district's needs. The schedule could not distinguish good teachers from bad, and it was unconnected to the district's strategic goals and to individual teachers' professional development.

Compounding these concerns, a profile of the district's teaching force indicated an impending crisis. A large group of young novices, an equally large group of older veterans nearing retirement age, and a much smaller group of midcareer teachers in their 30s and 40s constituted the district's teaching population. The implications were ominous: If the district could not retain and bolster its ranks of midcareer teachers, it would soon face an acute teacher shortage.

Over time, teachers, administrators, and school board members began to view their concerns about teacher attrition and their questions about the salary schedule as interrelated issues, and they sought a solution that would address both. They asked: How can compensation play a role in attracting and retaining high-quality teachers? This question led to a host of others, both practical and philosophical:

- How should we reward the early-career teacher who outperforms most veterans?
- Should the teacher evaluated as "unsatisfactory" still receive an annual step increase on the salary schedule?
- Should we invest additional resources in the competent teacher who pursues meaningful professional development and improves to a level of performance above the school district's expectations?
- Should we reward the teacher leader who contributes to the school beyond his or her own classroom, thereby positively influencing the performance of other teachers and indirectly contributing to the academic achievement of all students in the school?
- Should we reward the teacher who sets specific, measurable, and meaningful academic progress goals for his or her students, designs and implements strategies to achieve those goals, and then provides evidence of their achievement?
- How should we reward the teacher who achieves National Board certification?
- How can we recognize the contribution of an individual teacher to his or her students' academic growth, given that each student's achievement depends on the contributions of multiple teachers over several years?

Compensation Components: Strengthening the Salary Schedule

With the district's representative committee, we explored a range of current and proposed compensation systems, including group-based pay in Kentucky; a program for recognizing outstanding teachers in Douglas County, Colorado; a career ladder model proposal in Cincinnati, Ohio; a teacher leadership program in Maryland; and a pay-for-performance proposal in Pennsylvania. These initiatives, combined with our review of the research (most notably, Odden & Kelley, 1997), provided the rationale for pulling together a variety of effective compensation components into a single system for recognizing the value of teachers' work. The model we developed reflects our belief that a compensation system should recognize and reward a wide variety of the components that go into good teaching.

At the same time, we recognized that the traditional salary schedule remains popular for its perceived fairness and ease of administration. We also feared that abandoning the salary schedule could limit the district's ability to attract new teachers, who might be leery of a compensation system that differed so greatly from those of most school districts. Therefore, the traditional schedule remained the foundation on which we built our model.

As the district pursued implementation of the model, it recognized that substantive, lasting organizational change can take several years, and has therefore adopted a gradual approach, building on its existing salary schedule by introducing each component of the new model as a separate, stand-alone element.

Our compensation model has seven elements that work as bonus components to the base salary schedule. Figure 10.1 shows how the components fit together.

Components That Determine the Base Salary

Calculation of each teacher's total pay begins with the district's competitive base salary, which the teacher may increase through voluntary participation in the knowledge acquisition, skills block, and group-based pay components.

The *knowledge acquisition* component parallels the lanes in a conventional salary schedule that compensate teachers for graduate coursework and degrees.

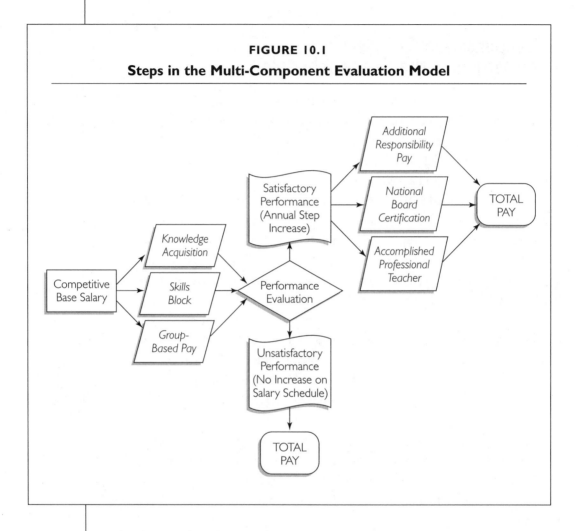

FIGURE 10.1

Steps in the Multi-Component Evaluation Model

The district identifies specific content and endorsement areas that qualify for tuition reimbursement: for example, coursework leading to a content-area graduate degree, coursework leading to a new subject-area endorsement, or coursework leading to endorsement in administration.

The *skills block* component offers additional pay for completion of a designated training program and the subsequent demonstration of mastery and application of the targeted skill. Unlike knowledge acquisition, skills blocks do not involve graduate credit hours or advanced degrees. Instead, they serve as a bonus compensation component available to all teachers each year. The school district identifies and provides the skills blocks, which are closely linked to school and district goals.

For example, a school district focused on improving literacy may provide specific training in the one-on-one reading intervention program Reading Recovery; a district developing its curriculum for gifted learners may provide training in teaching advanced placement courses; and a district concerned with equity issues may require completion of workshops on cultural competence. A teacher may pursue an advanced degree with a university while also completing skills block sessions with the school district.

Group-based pay is a bonus for a group of teachers who establish a specific improvement goal for a target group of students, develop and implement strategies to achieve the goal, and demonstrate the attainment of the goal. This type of performance-based pay has become more popular in education (Kelley, Heneman, & Milanowski, 2000). The district can organize teacher groups by school, multiple departments, sequential grade levels, teams, or a designated minimum number of teachers who share responsibility for a minimum number of students. The group's goals should define achievement as "value-added"—the improvement in achievement of the target group of students that can be attributed to the efforts of the defined group of teachers.

The Performance Evaluation Component

In this compensation model, the annual step increase associated with many salary schedules does not occur automatically. Instead, an *annual performance review*—a multisource evaluation system premised on defined teacher roles, student achievement goals, and substantive professional support—determines eligibility for the annual step increase.

Teachers who receive an "unsatisfactory" performance rating receive no annual step increase to their base salary. These teachers are frozen on the salary schedule, and they cannot participate in additional compensation options until they meet the goals of an improvement assistance plan.

Teachers whose performance is "satisfactory," however, have an annual step increase added to their base pay. They can also participate in additional compensation options, including additional responsibility pay, National Board certification, and pay through a locally designed program for the accomplished professional teacher.

Additional Compensation Options

Additional responsibility pay entails compensating teachers for performing designated extra duties. Although this concept is not new to education—coaches and activity sponsors, for example, have traditionally received stipends—our model expands the definition of additional responsibility pay to comprise three main categories. *Additional duty pay* includes coaching and club sponsorship. *School-based responsibility pay* compensates teachers for additional responsibilities deemed vital by their school, such as after-school tutoring, membership in school leadership teams, or the provision of professional development within the school. *Districtwide responsibility pay* compensates teachers for additional responsibilities deemed vital to the school district, such as membership on certain committees or task forces.

Compensation for **National Board certification** is another component of our model. The practice of rewarding teachers for earning this certification has become increasingly common among school districts and states. Such rewards typically take the form of up-front monetary assistance to support a teacher's effort to earn certification, or a bonus paid to a teacher over the duration of the certificate (10 years).

The **accomplished professional teacher program** is similar in concept to National Board certification. As a locally developed program unique to a given school district, this compensation component gives the district the latitude to adjust the program to align with its strategic goals. In addition, the accomplished professional teacher program emphasizes student achievement results, unlike National Board certification, which focuses primarily on process variables of teaching—that is, how the teacher teaches. A localized program recognizing accomplished professional teachers can focus more on output variables—the results of a teacher's teaching as demonstrated by student achievement. In considering this option, our district committee studied several value-added (that is, gain score) methods for demonstrating student achievement, including pre- and post-tests on curriculum-based assessments, standardized test results among comparable student populations, and assessment results on teacher-made criterion-referenced tests.

Conditions for Success

Budget constraints can pose significant obstacles to new program proposals. Consequently, any compensation reform initiative must focus on improving compensation within the boundaries of sustainable funding. Our component compensation model costs only 3 percent more than the current salary line.

The multiple-component compensation model offers many benefits. Combining a conventional salary schedule with a pay-for-performance system allows for both equity and competitiveness. The bonus components serve as attractive incentives for prospective employees and provide ongoing incentives for teachers to meet and exceed school district expectations. The knowledge acquisition and skills block components promote and reward professional growth and development. The accomplished professional teacher and group-based pay components link student achievement, teacher performance, teacher evaluation, and teacher compensation. The group-based pay component also encourages collaboration, a quality that improves teacher effectiveness (Kelley, Odden, Milanowski, & Heneman, 2000).

Implementing this approach, however, requires attention to a number of key issues within the district. First, many of the additional compensation components will require careful definitions of expectations, criteria, boundaries, and measurement strategies, all of which necessitate considerable administrative support and the collaborative involvement of all stakeholders, particularly teachers. Second, several of the compensation components require investment of professional development time and funding. Finally, as with any new initiative, the involvement of multiple stakeholders and attention to clear and regular communication are crucial to the implementation of change. The following actions will contribute to successful implementation of the compensation model:

- Make changes that are different, but not radical.
- Make sure that the teacher evaluation system is valid and reliable and can support the compensation system.
- Gain a critical mass of support among key stakeholder groups, such as school board members, district administrators, teachers, and community members.

- Communicate early and often.
- Make sure that the system is fair, easy to understand, and easy to administer.
- Ensure sustained political will.

Above all, remember that the purpose of the teacher compensation system is not just to attract and retain good teachers, but also to help them develop to their full potential.

References

Edwards, V. B. (Ed.). (2000). Quality counts 2000 [Special issue]. *Education Week, 29*(1).

Ingersoll, R. (2002). The teacher shortage: A case of wrong diagnosis and wrong prescription. *NASSP Bulletin, 86*(631).

Kelley, C., Heneman, H., & Milanowski, A. (2000). *School-based performance award programs, teacher motivation, and school performance: Findings from a study of three programs* (CPRE Research Report Series RR-44). Philadelphia: University of Pennsylvania, Consortium for Policy Research in Education.

Kelley, C., Odden, A., Milanowski, A., & Heneman, H. (2000). *The motivational effects of school-based performance awards* (CPRE Policy Briefs, RB-29). Philadelphia: University of Pennsylvania, Consortium for Policy Research in Education.

Odden, A., & Kelley, C. (1997). *Paying teachers for what they know and do: New and smarter compensation strategies to improve schools.* Thousand Oaks, CA: Corwin.

Rose, L. C., & Gallup, A. M. (2002). The 34th annual Phi Delta Kappa/Gallup poll of the public's attitudes toward the public schools. *Phi Delta Kappan, 84*(1), 41–56.

Stronge, J. H., & Tucker, P. D. (2002). *Handbook on teacher evaluation.* Larchmont, NY: Eye on Education.

11

How Career Paths Improve Job Satisfaction

John Schacter

John Schacter is vice president of research at the Milken Family Foundation, 1250 Fourth St., Santa Monica, CA 90401.

To most people, capital means a bank account, stock shares, assembly lines, or a physical production plant. Although these assets yield income and other outputs over time, their results pale in comparison to the capital that highly skilled and knowledgeable people generate (Becker, 1975). This capital, coined *human capital* by Nobel Laureate Gary Becker, now accounts for more than 75 percent of the wealth of the United States and 70 percent of the growth of its 100 largest companies (Milken, 2002).

Human capital is developed through education, and the effectiveness of a child's education depends on the quality of his or her classroom teachers. Unfortunately, school reforms often neglect the obvious importance of attracting, developing, and retaining high-quality teachers. In fact, of the more than 361 school reform ideas proposed in *Phi Delta Kappan* between 1987 and 1997, less than 1 percent have focused directly on improving teacher quality (Carpenter, 2000). Several studies, however, demonstrate that developing human capital in the teaching ranks should be the highest priority of every school reform.

Sanders and Horn's (1998) studies of teacher quality, for example, show that when 2nd grade students with initially similar achievement in mathematics reach 5th grade, the quality of the teachers they had separate their achievement scores by as many as 50 percentile points. Marzano's (2003) review of the research shows that if students in effective and ineffective teachers' classrooms take a test that one would expect half of the students to pass and half to fail, 81 percent of effective teachers' students pass, compared with 19 percent of the students assigned to ineffective teachers.

Finally, Thum's (in press) research indicates that the variance among teachers within a school—as measured by an individual classroom teacher's capacity to increase achievement—far surpasses the variance of achievement among schools. This finding affirms that teachers of varying quality are present in all schools, whether they are rich or poor, high-performing or low-performing. Together, these studies indicate that teachers are the single most important school-related factor responsible for a high-quality education. To provide students with a high-quality education, every school's main goal should be to improve the human capital in the teaching ranks.

Developing Human Capital

In other professions, management develops human capital by recognizing and promoting excellent employees; providing focused, ongoing training to improve individuals' competencies; creating an environment that facilitates teamwork; and assigning employees different salaries on the basis of their skills, knowledge, and responsibilities.

Most K–12 school policies, however, inhibit human capital development. Schools do not recognize, promote, or give additional authority and responsibility to teachers for excellent work; provide focused or ongoing professional development; or foster collaboration and teamwork among staff. Moreover, schools often assign all teachers the same salaries, irrespective of their competence, knowledge, or skills.

To encourage schools to cultivate human capital in the teaching profession, the Milken Family Foundation developed a comprehensive school reform model called the Teacher Advancement Program (TAP). In the 2002–2003 school year, 31 elementary schools in six states implemented the program, and 36 new schools in two new states will participate in 2003–2004. Five principles, formulated by Foundation President Lowell Milken in 1999, guide this comprehensive school reform model.

Establish Teacher Career Paths

Successful organizations encourage employees to specialize and develop particular competencies that are related to their interests, aptitudes, and roles (Elmore, 1999). These institutions provide opportunities for entrepreneurial and highly skilled personnel to take on new challenges, to advance, and to assume leadership positions with commensurate responsibility, authority, and compensation. Often, K–12 schools do not offer a career path. Every teacher—whether he or she has one year of experience or 20—holds the same position, engages in the same activities, and has the same authority and responsibilities (Johnson, 2001; Tyack & Hansot, 1980).

Rather than having all teachers perform the same job, Teacher Advancement Program schools restructure their personnel into a career continuum that ranges from inductee to career teacher to mentor and master teachers (see figure 11.1). This career path provides new opportunities for high-quality teachers to assume leadership roles, earn substantially more pay, and significantly contribute to setting the school's direction and course.

Master and mentor teachers in various disciplines and grade levels are instructional leaders who infuse and distribute their expertise across the staff. By pairing master teachers to share one classroom, the school creates release time for the master teachers to coach, conduct demonstration lessons, plan professional development, and act as a resource for curriculum, classroom management, and parent involvement strategies. Mentor teachers have 15 percent classroom release time for similar, albeit fewer, responsibilities. Creating an organizational structure that formally shares expert teachers' skills and creativity with all teachers in the school on a regular basis enhances the teaching quality and human capital of the faculty.

Provide Ongoing Professional Growth

Professional development in K–12 schools typically consists of half-day workshops led by outside consultants. Research on teacher learning, however, informs us that this delivery model is not effective. Those who study teachers explain that instruction is most likely to improve when teachers can

FIGURE 11.1

TAP Career Path for a 600-Student Elementary School

Career Path Position	Additional Pay	Number of Teachers	Classroom Release Time	Contract	Responsibilities
Master Teacher	$10,000	Four: two language arts and two math (one each for lower and upper elementary)	50 percent	11 months	• Designs and delivers professional development activities for the whole school, groups of teachers by grade and content level, and individual teachers. This professional development is aligned with content standards and has a direct impact on classroom instruction. • Determines the quarterly focus for each professional development group by grade or content level, and researches and gathers necessary learning materials. • Implements a weekly team-teaching demonstration lesson, coaching, and teacher evaluation schedule. • Serves as a resource for curriculum, assessment, instruction, classroom management, and parent volunteer strategies.

(continued)

FIGURE 11.1 (*continued*)

TAP Career Path for a 600-Student Elementary School

Career Path Position	Additional Pay	Number of Teachers	Classroom Release Time	Contract	Responsibilities
Mentor Teacher	$4,000	Four: One for each grade level	15 percent	10 months	• Assists master teacher in formulating quarterly professional development focus for groups of teachers by grade and content. • Coleads professional development group meetings with master teacher each week. • Implements a weekly team-teaching and teacher evaluation schedule. • Serves as a resource for developing curriculum, assessment, instruction, and classroom management strategies.
Career Teacher	None	16	None	9 months	• Participates in weekly professional development meetings that are organized by grade or content level. • Team teaches with a mentor or master teacher each quarter. • Reflects on knowledge, skills, and instructional practice; writes biannual professional growth plans.

(*continued*)

FIGURE 11.1 (*continued*)
TAP Career Path for a 600-Student Elementary School

Career Path Position	Additional Pay	Number of Teachers	Classroom Release Time	Contract	Responsibilities
Specialist	None	Two	None	9 months	• Participates in weekly professional development meetings. • Reflects on knowledge, skills, and instructional practice; writes biannual professional growth plans.

• Collaborate with professional peers,
• Concentrate on instruction and student outcomes for the specific content and context in which they teach,
• Have sustained opportunities to experiment with and receive feedback on specific teaching innovations, and
• Influence the substance and process of their professional development. (Desimone, Porter, Garet, Yoon, & Birman, 2002; King & Newmann, 2000; Newmann, Bryk, & Nagaoka, 2001)

These teacher-learning conditions are the cornerstone of Teacher Advancement Program schools' professional development. TAP's career path establishes a structure and schedule for master and mentor teachers to provide daily coaching, conduct classroom demonstration lessons, give regular feedback on specific teaching and learning innovations, and design learning opportunities that meet their fellow teachers' content and grade-level needs.

Require Performance-Based Accountability

Traditional schools do not adequately monitor teacher performance, rarely connect performance to professional growth, and almost never recognize and reward excellence. Single administrators perform most teacher evaluations on the basis of one annual classroom observation that focuses on classroom management, not effective instruction (Loup, Garland, Ellett, & Rugutt, 1996; National Association of Secondary School Principals, 2001).

In Teacher Advancement Program schools, several trained and certified evaluators—including the principal, master teachers, and mentor teachers—observe each teacher's classroom practice several times each year. These evaluators score classroom teaching against clearly defined instructional standards, and at five performance levels that range from exemplary to unsatisfactory (for more detail, see Schacter, Califano, Boch, & Bendotti, 2002). In addition to providing frequent classroom observations and coaching, TAP schools assess every teacher's performance on the basis of his or her students' achievement gains. Those who teach well, and whose students progress academically, receive rewards and promotions. Those who teach poorly, and whose students' achievement declines, receive sanctions.

Compensate Appropriately

In business, organizations pay employees different salaries according to their knowledge, skills, responsibilities, and value. Those with more responsibilities and authority, and with specialized skills in high-need fields, earn more. Most K–12 schools, however, pay every teacher the same and calculate all pay raises on the basis of years of experience and number of education credits (Odden & Kelley, 2002). Therefore, all teachers with the same experience and credits receive the same pay, no matter what they teach, how well they teach, how well their students achieve, or how many additional responsibilities they have (Odden, 2000).

In Teacher Achievement Program schools, market-driven compensation provides schools with the flexibility to compensate teachers differently on the basis of each teacher's performance, position (such as master, mentor, career, specialist, or inductee), and ability to fill a need, such as working in a hard-to-staff school or in a hard-to-staff subject area. Figure 11.2 shows how teachers receive compensation on the basis of the level of their skills, knowledge, and responsibilities (50 percent); their students' value-added achievement (20 percent); and the school's value-added achievement (30 percent).

FIGURE 11.2

Overview of the TAP Performance-Based Accountability and Compensation System

This accountability system consists of three assessments. Measurement instruments for career/specialist teachers and mentor teachers are portfolios, classroom observation, and value-added assessments. For master teachers, instruments are portfolios, classroom observation, and a survey of teachers he or she supervises.

Part I. Teacher Skills, Knowledge, and Responsibilities Assessment (50% of total score). This part of the assessment focuses on the individual teacher. The table below outlines the basics of the assessment process.

Key Elements of Part I Assessment	Career/Specialist Teacher	Mentor Teachers	Master Teachers
Number of instructional standards	21	23	25
Categories of standards (and contribution to Part I score)	• Designing and planning instruction (10%) • Instruction (75%) • The learning environment (10%) • Responsibilities: growing and developing professionally, reflecting on teaching (5%)	• Designing and planning instruction (10%) • Instruction (65%) • The learning environment (5%) • Responsibilities: staff development, mentoring, growing and developing professionally, reflecting on teaching (20%)	• Designing and planning instruction (10%) • Instruction (40%) • The learning environment (5%) • Responsibilities: staff development, instructional supervision, community involvement, school leadership through strategic planning; growing and developing professionally, reflecting on teaching (45%)
Evaluators (and contribution to Part I score)	• Self (10%) • Mentor teacher (20%) • Master teacher (35%) • Administrator (35%)	• Self (10%) • Mentor teacher (20%) • Master teacher (35%) • Administrator (35%)	• Self (10%) • Teachers under his or her supervision (40%) • Administrator (50%)
Minimum score required for satisfactory rating	2	3	4
Performance scale	1 through 5 [5 is best]	1 through 5 [5 is best]	1 through 5 [5 is best]

Part II. Classroom Value-Added Assessment (20% of total score). This part of the assessment focuses on what happens at the classroom level. Staff compare a teacher's achievement gains at the classroom level. Classes are scored on a scale of 1 to 5 as follows:

1 = 5th highest quintile
2 = 4th highest quintile
3 = 3rd highest quintile
4 = 2nd highest quintile
5 = highest quintile

Career/specialist teachers' class scores must be at least 2; mentor teachers' class scores must be at least 3; and master teachers' class scores must be at least 4.

Part III. Schoolwide Value-Added Assessment (30% of total score). This part of the assessment focuses on what happens across the entire school. Staff compare the achievement gains of the school with those of similar schools. Schools are scored on a scale of 1 to 5 as follows:

1 = 5th highest quintile
2 = 4th highest quintile
3 = 3rd highest quintile
4 = 2nd highest quintile
5 = highest quintile

Expand the Supply of High-Quality Teachers

Although schools may advertise locally for new teacher positions, teacher recruitment efforts rarely extend beyond the school district. Moreover, many states and districts place restrictions on hiring individuals who have not received traditional credentials. By contrast, Teacher Advancement Program schools expand teacher recruitment and outreach efforts by advertising mentor and master teacher positions that pay substantially more than the average teacher's salary, thereby encouraging high-quality teachers from other locales to apply. These schools also encourage districts and states to implement alternative certification policies that enable talented people to become teachers without facing unnecessary barriers to entering the profession. By recruiting aggressively, offering competitive salaries, and supporting alternative certification, these schools help expand the supply of high-quality teachers.

The Research

Our study analyzed the growth in student achievement in six Arizona schools that implemented the Teacher Advancement Program, compared with the achievement of students from similar schools in Arizona that did not implement these principles. In addition, we analyzed the effects of the Teacher Advancement Program on teacher attitudes and job satisfaction.

The six TAP schools ranged in size, from 411 students to approximately 1,400 students; percentage of students eligible for free lunch, from 15 percent to 93 percent; and location, from a large urban city to a small community.

The Arizona Department of Education conducted a cluster analysis of all Arizona schools to help us find schools of similar size, location, percentage of students eligible for free lunch, and levels of reading, math, and language achievement. The analysis found eight control schools that matched the TAP schools. Figure 11.3 reports the Spring 2000 baseline achievement data, percentage of students eligible for free or reduced-price lunch, school size, and school configuration of the TAP schools and their matched controls.

Although the six schools implemented all five reform principles, we found considerable variability in the degree of implementation. To account for and measure these differences, we designed a TAP implementation instrument that enabled teams of evaluators to visit the TAP schools and rate implementation on 39 items using a 5-point Likert scale. The implementation scores have a possible range from 39 to 195, with 39 indicating extremely low levels of implementation and 195 indicating extremely high levels of implementation. Using these scores, we were able to analyze how the level of implementation affected the level of student achievement.

We also assessed teachers' job satisfaction, their attitudes toward the five principles of the Teacher Advancement Program, and their satisfaction with the level of professional collaboration in their schools. In 2001, 85 percent of the teachers responded, and 78 percent responded in 2002.

To analyze student achievement, we used the total reading, language, and mathematics scale scores for grades 2–6 of the Stanford 9 Achievement Tests. We designed a multilevel, value-added statistical model to make the comparisons between TAP and control schools (see Schacter et al., 2002 and Thum, in press, for statistical model specifications).

Student Achievement Results

Our research examined the overall effect of the Teacher Advancement Program on student achievement across multiple schools, in individual schools, and among teachers. In addition to reporting achievement at these levels compared with controls, we used our implementation data to explain some of the variability in achievement gains across TAP schools. The results were encouraging.

TAP Schools improve student achievement. Our analyses demonstrate that all TAP schools made improvements in student achievement, both in the first and second years of reform. In 2000–2001, the highest-performing TAP school, at a 95 percent confidence level, made a 23 percent gain, and the lowest-performing TAP school made a 5 percent gain. In 2001–2002, the highest-performing TAP school made a 28 percent gain, and the lowest-performing TAP school made a 2 percent gain. The average TAP school gain each year was 11.5 percent, or 23 percent over two years.

TAP Schools outperform comparable schools. When compared with control schools, TAP schools gained significantly more than control schools did in reading, language, and mathematics, in both 2000–2001 and 2001–2002. In 2000–2001, at a 95 percent level of confidence, TAP schools outgained control schools by 6 percent, and in 2001–2002, TAP schools outperformed

FIGURE 11.3

TAP and Comparison School 2000 Baseline Demographic and Achievement Data

School	Total Achievement Percentile Rank	Reading Percentile Rank	Math Percentile Rank	Enrolled Students	Percentage of Students Eligible for Free Lunch	Grades
All TAP schools	41	39	42	3,319	59	K–8
All control schools	39	37	41	7,055	64	K–8
TAP 1[1]	68	69	72	725	15	K–8
Control	62	61	64	711	25	K–8
TAP 2	37	36	37	650	93	K–6
Control	39	36	40	935	92	K–6
Control	37	33	40	645	85	K–6
TAP 3[2]	66	66	65	600	52	K–4
Control	52	49	53	860	53	K–4
Control	45	44	45	575	64	K–4
TAP 4	45	42	48	1,369	62	K–6
Control	47	45	50	959	66	K–6
Control	47	45	52	1,092	55	K–6
Control	45	41	50	1,211	83	K–6
TAP 5[3]	63	61	66	411	46	K–4
TAP 6[3]	49	49	49	854	70	3–8

[1] There are a limited number of K–8 schools in the state. TAP 1, which is a charter school, is compared with a noncharter school with a K–8 configuration. On the basis of the state's cluster analysis, this school was the best possible match.
[2] There are a limited number of K–4 schools in the state. The best matching K–4 school was dropped because the school became a TAP school in 2001. On the basis of the state's cluster analysis, these K–4 controls were the best possible match.
[3] Control schools have yet to be identified.

control schools by 7 percent. Over the course of two years, TAP schools out-gained their controls by approximately 13 percent.

Individual TAP Schools outperform the control schools. When comparing each TAP school with its individual control school, the results demonstrated that in both 2000–2001 and 2001–2002, three of the four TAP schools gained significantly more in reading, language, and mathematics than did their control schools.

TAP teachers produce more student achievement gains. A greater proportion of teachers in TAP schools produce student learning gains when compared with teachers in control schools. The proportion of teachers in TAP schools that produced student achievement gains was significantly greater than the proportion of teachers producing student achievement gains in control schools, thereby demonstrating that TAP schools did, indeed, improve teacher quality and human capital in their teaching ranks.

Better TAP implementation equals more gains. TAP schools with higher implementation ratings produce greater student achievement gains than do TAP schools that implement the five principles less rigorously. Rigorous implementation included competitive and broad hiring processes for master and mentor teachers; clear and differentiated responsibilities for master, mentor, and career teachers; high-quality master and mentor teachers who possess exemplary instructional skills and the ability to competently lead the school's professional development; ample shared professional development time during the school day (at least 2 hours per week); high-quality teacher evaluation; commensurate compensation for master and mentor teachers; and a rigorous performance pay system in which all teachers can earn significant yearly awards.

Two TAP schools had high implementation ratings, one had a moderate rating, and two had moderate to low scores. We found that the two TAP schools with high implementation ratings outgained their control schools by approximately 22 percent each year. Conversely, the school with the lowest implementation level made considerably less progress, even though it still produced achievement gains.

Teacher Satisfaction and Attitudes Survey Results

Increasing teacher morale makes teaching more enjoyable and creates a more positive and effective learning environment for students (Black, 2001; Lumsden, 1998; Miller, 1981). We measured teacher support for the Teacher Advancement Program principles, and we measured for feelings of collegiality, teamwork, and school support.

After one year of implementing the Teacher Advancement Program, 74 percent of teachers responded that they felt a strong sense of collegial support and teamwork, and the majority of teachers strongly supported the program's multiple careers paths, professional development, accountability system, and performance pay.

After implementing TAP's five principles for two years, the majority of teachers continued to strongly support the program's multiple career paths professional development, and felt a strong sense of collegial support and teamwork. Far fewer teachers, however, strongly supported the program's performance pay (see figure 11.4).

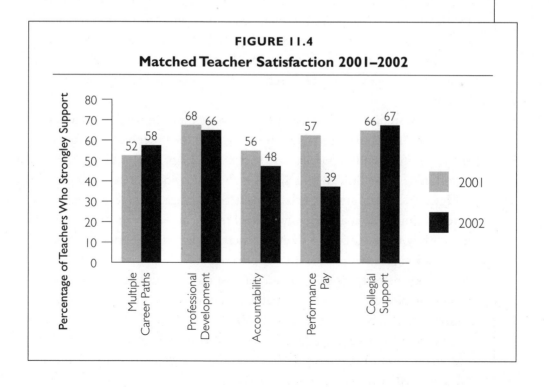

FIGURE 11.4
Matched Teacher Satisfaction 2001–2002

We should note that although schools had practiced implementing TAP principles in 2001, they did not incorporate rewards and consequences until 2002. Also, we administered the teacher survey three months before teachers received their performance pay awards. Thus, the teachers had just undergone a year of rigorous accountability and had not yet received additional compensation for their performance and effort.

The apparent drop in support for performance pay, however, does not appear to be creating a competitive school environment in which teamwork, sharing, and collegiality are discouraged; as many as 70 percent of teachers in TAP schools reported a very strong sense of teacher support and collegiality.

What Do the Results Mean?

Despite variation in size, location, socioeconomic status, and student achievement levels, all TAP schools posted achievement gains in both years that they implemented the reform, and they significantly outgained comparison schools by a total of 13 percent over two years.

Although the results of TAP are generally positive, the level of implementation of TAP appeared to play a large role in terms of how successful each individual school was in increasing student achievement. TAP schools with high implementation scores produced considerably larger student achievement gains than TAP schools that moderately implemented the reform.

Recent studies on comprehensive school reform demonstrate that implementation "tends to be variable across sites, and the outcomes also vary considerably" (Berends, Bodilly, & Kirby, 2002, p. 170). Our analyses, unfortunately, confirm this finding. Of the four schools that implemented TAP for two years, student achievement gains ranged from 8 percent to 51 percent. Studies of comprehensive school reform also show that the reform is more likely to be successful when teachers support it, the principal demonstrates strong leadership, the district provides stable and committed support, the school receives ongoing financial assistance and training, and small schools implement the reform (Berends, Bodilly, & Kirby, 2002; Berends, Chun, Schuyler, Stockly, & Briggs, 2002).

In the high-achieving TAP schools, most of these components were present. In the lowest-performing TAP school, the principal was replaced, the district showed little commitment to the reform, teachers only marginally supported TAP, and the school was large—a K–6 elementary school with approximately 1,400 students.

Our study did have some limitations. We matched each TAP school to similar controls rather than conduct a randomized trial. Such a trial would have randomly selected schools for implementing TAP and compared them with schools that had been randomly selected as control schools—an approach that would provide the highest-quality data on which to base generalizations about our results.

A second limitation of this study was that we did not collect data to evaluate what was occurring in control schools. Control schools in Arizona may have implemented one or more of the TAP principles at varying degrees of quality. By not collecting such data on control schools, we are unaware of whether control schools implemented one or more TAP-like principles.

Finally, this study of six schools and two years of data is, by definition, preliminary. Although these results are positive, more TAP schools and more years of student data will be required to come to sound conclusions of the impact of the Teacher Advancement Program.

Nonetheless, our preliminary data suggest that implementing these five principles can increase student achievement in Title I and non-Title I schools, in initially high-achieving and initially low-achieving schools, and in schools in large and small urban communities. But, as is the case with many comprehensive school reform efforts, our results illustrate that high-quality implementation is essential to achieve successful and lasting outcomes.

References

Becker, G. (1975). *Human capital: A theoretical and empirical analysis with special reference to education.* Chicago: University of Chicago Press.

Berends, M., Bodilly, S., & Kirby, S. N. (2002). Looking back over a decade of whole-school reform: The experience of new American schools. *Phi Delta Kappan, 84,* 168–175.

Berends, M., Chun, J., Schuyler, G., Stockly, S., & Briggs, R. J. (2002). *Challenges of conflicting reforms: Effects of New American Schools in a high poverty district.* Santa Monica, CA: Rand.

Black, S. (2001). Morale matters: When teachers feel good about their work, research shows, student achievement rises. *American School Board Journal, 188,* 40–43.

Carpenter, W. A. (2000). Ten years of silver bullets: Dissenting thoughts on education reform. *Phi Delta Kappan, 81,* 383–389.

Desimone, L., Porter, A. C., Garet, M. S., Yoon, K. S., & Birman, B. F. (2002). Effects of professional development on teachers' instruction: Results from a three-year longitudinal study. *Education Evaluation and Policy Analysis, 24,* 81–112.

Elmore, R. F. (1999). Building a new structure for school leadership. *American Educator, 23,* 6–13.

Johnson, S. M. (2001). Can professional certification for teachers reshape teaching as a career? *Phi Delta Kappan, 82,* 393–399.

King, B. M., & Newmann, F. M. (2000). Will teacher learning advance school goals? *Phi Delta Kappan,* 576–580.

Loup, K. S., Garland, J. S., Ellett, C. D., & Rugutt, J. K. (1996). Ten years later: Findings from a replication of a study of teacher evaluation practices in our 100 largest school districts. *Journal of Personnel Evaluation in Education, 10,* 203–226.

Lumsden, L. (1998). Teacher morale. *ERIC Digest, 120.*

Marzano, R. J. (2003). *What works in schools: Translating research into action.* Alexandria, VA: Association for Supervision and Curriculum Development.

Milken, L. (2002). *The growth of the Teacher Advancement Program.* Santa Monica, CA: Milken Family Foundation.

Miller, W. C. (1981). Staff morale, school climate, and education productivity. *Educational Leadership, 38,* 483–486.

National Association of Secondary School Principals. (2001). *Priorities and barriers in high school leadership: A survey of principals.* Reston, VA: Author.

Newmann, F. M., Bryk, A. S., & Nagaoka, J. K. (2001). *Authentic intellectual work and standardized tests: Conflict or coexistence.* Chicago: Consortium on Chicago School Research.

Odden, A. (2000). New and better forms of teacher compensation are possible. *Phi Delta Kappan, 81,* 361–366.

Odden, A., & Kelley, C. (2002). *Paying teachers for what they know and do: New and smarter compensation strategies to improve schools* (2nd ed.). Thousand Oaks, CA: Corwin.

Sanders, W. L., & Horn, S. P. (1998). Research findings from the Tennessee value-added assessment system (TVAAS) database: Implications for educational evaluation and research. *Journal of Personnel Evaluation in Education, 12,* 247–256.

Schacter, J., Califano, L., Boch, J., & Bendotti, M. (2002). Quality teachers: Defining and developing them. *Instructional Leader, 15,* 1–10.

Schacter, J., Schiff, T., Thum, Y. M., Fagnano, C., Solmon, L. C., & Milken, L. (2002). *The impact of the teacher advancement program on student achievement and teacher attitudes.* Santa Monica, CA: Milken Family Foundation.

Thum, Y. M. (in press). Estimating teacher productivity using a multivariate, multi-level value-added model. *Sociological Research Methods*.

Tyack, D., & Hansot, E. (1980). From social movement to professional management: An inquiry into the changing character of leadership in public education. *American Journal of Education, 88*, 291–319.

12

Moving Up

Excellent Teachers Who Leave the Classroom

J. F. McCullers

J. F. McCullers is program administrator for grants and program development for the School District of Lee County, Florida. He can be reached via e-mail at jeffm@lee.k12.fl.us.

Several years ago, after a long and successful career as a high school English teacher, I left teaching to become an administrator. Since then, my assignments in various staff development, personnel, and grants positions have been rewarding and enjoyable. Like many administrators, however, I've struggled with a nagging sense that when I left the classroom, I left behind something wonderful.

Part of my current assignment involves directing our yearlong "grow-your-own-administrator" inservice program, called Leading Edge. This program helps classroom teachers investigate leadership roles and opportunities. Like many other districts across the country, we have experienced a growing shortage of qualified school administrators. The goal of the Leading Edge program is to make transitions from the classroom into administration more orderly, efficient, and successful for those whose talents and interests qualify them as potential administrators.

A group of about a dozen current teachers who are interested in leadership roles outside the classroom meets monthly. The program does not attempt to simulate an education leadership program that one might find at a university, but instead provides a way to help move theory into practice. We look at policy issues, current trends in leadership and organizational design, and practical day-to-day problems that school administrators face.

My involvement with Leading Edge heightened my curiosity about why some of our best teachers abandoned their classrooms to assume other roles in the school community. After a rousing discussion or two on this topic with my Leading Edge group, I decided to ask a number of our former high-performing teachers—who now serve in instructional support roles as administrators, teachers-on-assignment, or school-based specialists—why they left the classroom. Here are the stories of four of these former superstar teachers.

The Opportunity to Help More Students with Less Stress

Cheryl Young came to teaching through an alternative certification program after a successful career as a music therapist. Her first teaching assignment placed her in a portable classroom with low-performing, inner-city high school students with a variety of learning and behavioral disorders.

As the fourth teacher assigned to this class in less than two years, she found the work both rewarding and frustrating. For the next six years, she drew on her skills as a therapist to help frustrated, rebellious teenagers learn to cope with their serious academic challenges. Like hundreds of thousands of teachers before her, she came to love her students and considered her work something she was called to do. However, she began to question how long she could maintain the emotional strength necessary to help her students succeed. Things came to a head when one student was shot by another a short distance from her classroom door. Shortly thereafter, she requested a transfer to a suburban middle school.

At first, her new assignment as the "anchor, team leader, spirit-driver, and problem-solver" on a teaching team was her "dream job." She found a greater sense of camaraderie with her colleagues and greater support from parents, but also noticed that the turnover rate on this successful team was quite high. Many of the most effective teachers were lured away to other assignments within the first year, and she found herself continually training new team members. As this pattern continued unabated, she began to lose confidence and enthusiasm. Eventually, she "burned out" and looked for another role in which she could continue to help children without feeling so emotionally drained herself.

Cheryl's decision to leave the classroom was less difficult than she had feared—perhaps because she was professionally prepared and emotionally ready for her new position as a behavioral specialist. Compared with classroom teaching, this position enables her to help more students, provides more authentic and lasting collegial relationships, increases her ability to make a difference in the school, and gives her more manageable responsibilities. She feels professionally renewed, and has recently entered a doctoral program. Cheryl has no desire to return to the stress of teaching emotionally handicapped classes.

The "Tough Trade-Off": Student Contact vs. Greater Influence

Like several of the former teachers in this group, Ann Cole sees the main reason for her decision to move into administration as the opportunity to have a greater influence on school and district practices. Ann had been a popular elementary school counselor who worked with students on stranger danger, peer mediation, conflict resolution, character education, and child abuse prevention programs. Highly regarded by classroom teachers as a key member of her school's instructional team, Ann enjoyed the love of her students and the appreciation of her principal.

Ann was not eager to leave her instructional role. Like Cheryl, however, she had talents and interests that qualified her for roles in education outside the classroom. Her success in working with students was so apparent that the district's guidance coordinator and a consulting university professor encouraged her to consider a district position where she could help other counselors achieve the same success.

Eventually, she found an ideal opportunity and left her school to work in the district office as a teacher on special assignment. Instead of conducting programs for just one school, she now works districtwide to encourage and facilitate partnerships between social service agencies and schools. Like Cheryl, she feels professionally rejuvenated by the change. But she describes the decision to give up direct student contact in order to gain greater influence on the whole system as a "tough trade-off." Although she feels satisfied that she made the right professional decision, she misses the students she left behind.

Trying to Preserve the Classroom Connection

Most of these former teachers try to preserve and nurture the student contact that they enjoyed in the classroom. For example, Joni Logan taught high school Latin for 18 years before deciding to leave the classroom for administration. She grew up wanting to become a teacher, and she enjoyed kindling in students her own love for learning. Joni was one of those people who seem naturally gifted in the art of teaching, and her lessons in this "dead" language were full of life and excitement.

Joni began her teaching career in 1967, in the era of school desegregation and the Vietnam War. During this time of great social change, Joni considered herself a classroom innovator. Along the way, she taught in new high schools, experimented with modular scheduling, coached intern teachers, and served as a school activity director. Even after earning her master's degree, Joni didn't seriously consider leaving the classroom for three more years.

But Joni was curious about what she might be able to do as an administrator. She had heard rumors that the certification requirements for administrators would soon change, and was concerned that her opportunity to try her hand at administration might slip away. So she put in a single application for a position as a high school dean of students. To her surprise, she was selected.

She "had never even written a referral before" and learned much in her new position. In her ensuing years as a school administrator, she always felt connected to the classroom. She occasionally taught a section or two of Latin in addition to her administrative duties. Later, when she became a principal, she enjoyed visiting classes and learning about new methods and curriculums.

Now a district administrator, Joni is acutely and uncomfortably aware that she has moved farther away from the classroom—and she misses the students. She still goes to football games, academic awards ceremonies, and "pretty much anything else" to which a school invites her.

A Mission to Make Schools Better for Students

Like Joni, Nancy Graham believes that she was "born to be a teacher." She recalls playing school as a child: Working with the chalkboard she got for Christmas when she was 8, she would conduct class on her carport and would somehow get all her playmates seated and involved in learning actual lessons.

After several years working with a youth ministry program, and then as a private school teacher, Nancy took a position teaching in a public high school. The job offer was contingent on her promise that she could lead students in producing a school yearbook, although she had no experience in high school journalism. That risky promise led to an exemplary career. Nancy discovered a talent for making difficult academic concepts come alive, and she established a reputation as a "tough" teacher who found a way to help every student succeed. Nancy soon became the head of the English department, and other schools often called on her to present workshops on her successful methods and materials.

Over the years, Nancy came to see herself as an advocate for high school students. She had grown to genuinely love these students, but she sensed that some of their teachers failed to share that same spirit of caring. She believes that she had "no choice" but to leave the classroom for an administrative position, to fulfill her personal mission of making school life better for students.

Nancy's administrative career has been as successful as her teaching career. As an assistant principal and then principal, she has continued to pursue her mission of making schools into the kinds of places that students need. This requires a broad perspective and some hard decisions, and Nancy describes the principalship as a "lonely role."

Walking the halls of her school during a class change, Nancy engages student after student much as a teacher would: looking for an angle, a point of common interest, a way in. With laughter and banter she keeps up with the daily progress of each of "her" students. When the bell rings, however, the doors close and Nancy walks back to her office and continues with her mission.

The Way It's Supposed to Work

Although they were successful as teachers, each of these four women found some reason to leave her instructional role. Anyone who has taught for a while can come up with another list of extraordinary teachers who now work in education outside the classroom. Of the 20 finest teachers I knew just a few years ago, only two remain in the classroom. Some have left the teaching profession altogether, but most became administrators.

Of course, that's the way it's supposed to work. Some of our classroom teachers will inevitably move up into administrative roles or move over into other instructional positions such as guidance counselor, media specialist, behavioral specialist, or technology specialist. After all, we do need principals and supervisors in our schools who have had teaching experience.

In considering education policies that affect teachers' careers, however, we should keep in mind that the skills, traits, knowledge, and talents that make someone an exceptional teacher do not always make that person an exceptional administrator. For example, teachers need to be minutely concerned and utterly fluent with the complex needs of individual students, whereas principals need to understand and predict the needs of hundreds or thousands of current and future students.

With this in mind, we should not automatically assume that the logical career path of a great teacher will lead that teacher out of the classroom. Great organizations work hard to place an employee in the *right* position rather than the next position up, according to a recent Gallup study.[1]

We also need to think about the optimum balance between keeping the best teachers in the classroom, and enabling those with the desire and talent to move on to administrative roles. Such "grow-your-own" programs as our Leading Edge group can help teachers explore their options and decide whether they want to move into administration. In addition, we should encourage teachers to take advantage of existing opportunities for leadership that do not involve leaving the classroom. In our district, for example, many teachers provide meaningful leadership through professional associations, through the activities of the local affiliate of the National Board for Professional Teaching Standards, and by serving on various district and school advisory committees.

Another example of teacher leadership is the Florida League of Teachers, a group of exemplary teachers (mostly those recognized as district or state teacher of the year) who provide coaching, mentoring, training, and development services to their colleagues across the state. With nearly 150 members, the League of Teachers enables teachers to serve as highly visible and effective leaders without leaving their classrooms and students.

Districts can also provide teacher leadership opportunities through career ladders. Although such programs often face barriers, such as resistance from teachers' organizations or insufficient funding, the idea has some promise. Each school could routinely have on staff a handful of highly effective master teachers whose duties would include leadership in key instructional areas.

---

[1] Buckingham, M., & Coffman, C. (1999). *First, break all the rules: What the world's greatest managers do differently.* New York: Simon & Schuster.

These teachers could provide professional development and mentoring to new teachers, review and improve lesson plans and instructional designs, model effective instruction, and work directly as peers with classroom teachers.

The Importance of Asking Questions

Working with my Leading Edge group has raised many questions. Some of these exceptional teachers will leave their classrooms and go on to other positions, mostly in administration. Maybe that's good and maybe it's not, but I'm convinced that the group participants benefit by reflecting on what they hope to gain and what they will give up in making such a move. If they decide to leave the classroom, I hope that they'll follow the example of Cheryl, Ann, Joni, and Nancy, and strive to maintain the connection with students that made them great teachers.

13

My Journey to National Certification

Mary C. Brennan

Mary C. Brennan teaches 4th grade at Pritchett Elementary School, 200 Horatio Blvd., Buffalo Grove, IL 60089. She can be reached via e-mail at mbrennan@aptakisic.k12.il.us.

On a beautiful day in May 2001, I was so busy taking a test that I was oblivious to the spring weather. As I was leaving the assessment center, a young man just entering the building commented, "You look confident." Before I could answer, the testing proctor replied, "Well, she should be. She just spent eight hours writing about what she does every day." As I thought about his remark, I realized that the journey of self-discovery I had undergone in getting certified by the National Board for Professional Teaching Standards (NBPTS) had made me a confident professional.

I pursued NBPTS certification for both professional and personal reasons: to show how challenging teaching is and validate its professional status. I also wanted to demonstrate to the public a professional commitment to excellence, and help provide a catalyst for broader education reforms to support teaching (Sykes, 1989).

The Challenge

I have been a teacher in the early grades of elementary school for 13 years. For the past several years, I have taught a 4th grade class of approximately 26 students in a K–4 school of 530 students in a suburb northwest of Chicago.

I entered the teaching profession in my 30s after a successful business career. As a young person, I had resisted teaching—my parents and numerous relatives were teachers, and I wanted to be different. But even in business, I found myself gravitating toward the training department. When I became a teacher, I began to understand the passion that had kept my father in the classroom for so many years. I found that same passion in myself, but now I wanted a new challenge. I thought about going into administration, but I knew that I wanted to work directly with students. I thought about pursuing a doctorate, but my two college-age children and two more at home made such a plan difficult. National certification matched my needs, especially because the state of Illinois was willing to pay the application fee and offered support workshops and mentors for qualified candidates. I have always been eager to take on challenges, and certification offered a challenge that would meet my career goals.

In July, when I received a letter congratulating me on qualifying for state funding, I was well into the summer syndrome of many teachers—anything seems possible during the summer months. Despite warnings that certification involved a major time commitment—requiring as much as two hours of work daily—I made my lofty plans. Forewarned but optimistic, I thought to myself, "You always do things quickly; surely it won't take that many hours." It did! But it was well worth the effort.

In August, when a large box filled with information on the certification process arrived, I felt overwhelmed. The box contained rules, guidelines, standards, directions, articles to read, labels, and detailed instructions about saving the box and packing my materials in it when I submitted my work. The box arrived just as I was preparing to start a new school year, and I began to wonder why I had chosen this particular challenge. But I had made a commitment, so I cleared a drawer in my file cabinet, bought a huge binder, and thought, "Now what?"

In early October, at Illinois's regional meeting for candidates, I was impressed with the commitment and professionalism of past recipients and my fellow candidates. Nervous energy filled the room as we shared our questions, concerns, and tips for beginning the portfolio portion of the certification process. We found support networking through meeting in formal or informal groups, and consulting the NBPTS Web site. We wished one another good luck and agreed to meet again in early May to prepare for the assessment component of certification. When I returned home, I decided to join a local university's support group for guiding and supporting teachers through this process, a decision that enriched my journey tremendously.

Analysis and Reflection

Certification clearly supports learning in the classroom. My journey involved intense analysis and reflection. It validated what I do in my 4th grade classroom and challenged me in more ways than I thought possible. The habits I developed during this certification process have become routine today. For example, because I had to use samples of student work to share and demonstrate student learning, I developed the habit of keeping better anecdotal records and saving student work for analysis. Another challenge during the certification process was using videotape for my portfolio. I soon saw the benefits of this tool, both for my own analysis and for student reflection and learning, and now the camera is a frequent visitor in my classroom. At one point during the year, my principal asked, "Do the parents in your room realize the outstanding instruction their children are receiving as you go through this certification process?" By looking carefully at learning and continually challenging myself to do more, I was also challenging my students. As I modeled the learning process, my students followed my lead. The process underscored the belief that "professional learning and student learning go hand in hand" (Sagor, 1995, p. 27).

In my weekly support group, eight outstanding teachers shared their practices and challenged themselves to meet the standards of excellence in teaching established by the NBPTS. One of the greatest problems that many teachers face is a sense of isolation. We never really know what the teacher next door is doing. We may share activities and ideas, but we rarely open up our practice to scrutiny and to the kind of collaborative work that this group undertook. Our facilitator, one of the first certified NBPTS teachers, guided us through the process of completing our portfolios and preparing for our written assessments.

Our first portfolio entries documented our professional development experiences and community involvement. I included the work that I had done with student council and business partnerships. I described how our student council participated in community projects, such as "Make a Difference Day," which involved sponsoring a food drive for a local food pantry. I highlighted our participation with community members in an environmental program that resulted in our obtaining an Earth flag for our school. These entries underscored how teachers' professional growth enriches the classroom and how home, school, and community are all involved in educating students.

It was rewarding to carefully examine my entire professional development and to think about my future direction. I solidified my commitment to becoming a career teacher and to serving as a mentor and teacher leader. Equally powerful was learning about other teachers' accomplishments. Leslie, a junior high school math teacher, makes home visits to students who need extra help. The students of Jennifer, a 3rd grade teacher, design and play math games with senior citizens. These efforts should be recognized and valued.

My portfolio also required entries about specific classroom activities in four areas: language arts, math, science, and building a classroom community. I became a "kid watcher" and teacher researcher, constantly probing, questioning, listening, noticing, and noting (VanDeWeghe, 1992).

My entries on classroom activities also showed how to embed standards in instruction. For example, my entry on science demonstrated how I took an interdisciplinary theme—the changing earth—and engaged students in investigating such issues as weathering and erosion. This unit matched one of our state's learning goals, which is to understand the fundamental concepts, principles, and interconnections among the physical and Earth sciences. I showed the value of science instruction that is 60 percent hands-on and inquiry-based.

I also shared my analysis of two students' needs through samples of their work and demonstrated how I differentiated instruction to meet each student's individual needs. One student, a high achiever with a need to consider others' perspectives more carefully, benefited from opportunities to develop his interpersonal skills through group investigations. The other student, who needed more time to understand the material, benefited from opportunities to explore and "mess around" with the lesson's materials.

The work I did on my portfolio served as "an exhibition of my efforts, progress, and achievements in one or more areas" (Paulson, Paulson, & Meyer, 1991, p. 60). It was also an instructional tool that informed the daily learning that was taking place in my classroom. I shared my drafts and entries with students so that they could collaborate with me on this learning process. My students saw how hard I worked. They knew that they could help me fulfill my goal to become the best possible teacher.

When we completed our portfolios, my support group had a packing party to prepare our boxes for mailing. As we packed, took pictures, and enjoyed refreshments, we felt a tremendous sense of accomplishment for having completed this part of the process.

Demonstrating Excellence

Now it was time to prepare for our written assessments. When the Illinois group met in May, a panel of teachers certified by the NBPTS shared their experiences, provided helpful tips, and offered encouragement. The best advice I received was to write about what I do every day and about the decisions I make in the interest of student learning.

In my weekly support group, we shared resources and practiced for this part of the process. The NBPTS provided sample tests, the support group compared notes, and each of us also consulted the online tutorial for writing entries. During the 90-minute practice assessments, we analyzed such materials as student work samples, assessment records, instructional resource materials, and professional reading. We diagnosed student learning and planned instruction to meet specific needs, goals, and assumptions (National Board for Professional Teaching Standards, 2003).

My principal shared her observation of my readiness for this assessment when she wrote, "Your input at our social studies staff development meeting demonstrated your competency at curriculum design, backwards mapping, and constructivist learning. Your peers respected your input, and you were able to model deep understanding of the process." The tasks that we undertook in our written assessments exemplified purposeful performance assessment. In each of the entries, I was able to "create a rich and full picture of my growth over time, with a cumulative sense of what I know" (Diez, 2000, p. 49). I became involved professionally and emotionally; I was able to write from my heart.

As I encourage others to participate in the process of NBPTS certification, I am quick to point out that the process does not involve adding another layer to instruction. Instead, the process captures in words what we actually do every day and sets high standards for all teachers (see Figure 13.1). Putting together a portfolio integrates theory with everyday instruction. It guides us as we work with students. It made my instruction stronger, challenged my creativity, and afforded me opportunities to be reflective and analytical. The process helped me systematically capture and understand the learning that is taking place in the classroom. My efforts serve as a powerful model for my students and their learning. The public needs to see what we are doing to demonstrate the excellence that abounds in our craft. We need to celebrate our accomplishments.

FIGURE 13.1
The NBPTS Core Beliefs

Teachers

- Are committed to students and their learning
- Know the subjects they teach and how to teach those subjects to students
- Are responsible for managing and monitoring their student learning
- Think systematically about their practice and learn from experience
- Are members of learning communities

Source: National Board for Professional Teaching Standards (2002, pp. 3–4).

So, yes, I did feel confident leaving the assessment center. I smiled, wished the young man good luck, and continued on my way. I had spent the day thinking on my feet—that special skill that we teachers possess. I also felt relief. I had completed a journey begun the summer before, a journey that represents me: an accomplished teacher.

References

Diez, M. (2000). Teachers, assessment, and the standards movement. *Education Week, 19*(34), 45, 49.

National Board for Professional Teaching Standards. (2002). *What teachers should know and be able to do.* Arlington, VA: Author. Available: www.nbpts.org/pdf/coreprops.pdf

National Board for Professional Teaching Standards. (2003). *View exercise descriptions.* Arlington, VA: Author. Available: www.nbpts.org/candidates/acob/2_exerdesc.html#

Paulson, F., Paulson, P., & Meyer, C. (1991). What makes a portfolio a portfolio? *Educational Leadership, 48*(5), 60–63.

Sagor, R. (1995). Overcoming the one-solution syndrome. *Educational Leadership, 52*(7), 24–27.

Sykes, G. (1989). National certification for teachers: A dialogue. *NEA Today, 7*(6), 6–12.

VanDeWeghe, R. (1992). What teachers learn from "kid watching." *Educational Leadership, 49*(7), 49–52.

14

Going for the Gold

Frank R. Petruzielo

Frank R. Petruzielo is superintendent of the Cherokee County School District, P. O. Box 769, Canton, GA 30169. He can be reached via e-mail at dr.p@cherokee.k12.ga.us.

What are the most important decisions that district school superintendents have to make? The quality of curriculum, discipline, and school construction are vital for a school district to function at a high level, but most superintendents know that their top challenge is to attract and retain good teachers. They know that teacher quality has the greatest impact on student achievement (Prince, 2002), that districts must compete with other districts that share the same priorities, and that schools must go up against business and other industries' efforts to attract and keep talented employees (Marx, 2000).

Having worked in public education for 35 years (12 as a superintendent), I am familiar with this challenge. Before becoming superintendent of schools in Cherokee County, Georgia, in 1999, I led the exceptionally large school districts of Broward County, Florida, and Houston, Texas. Cherokee, a suburb 30 miles north of Atlanta, is the 36th fastest-growing county in the United States. Its population has increased by more than 57 percent during the past 10 years, and experts predict that it will increase another 37 percent by 2010. In all three districts, whether I served the residents of an affluent suburb or those of an urban center, my job's greatest challenge has been to recommend policies and implement strategies for developing an excellent teaching force.

In Georgia, my first step was to work with the Cherokee County Board of Education to set personnel issues as the top priority. With the collaboration and support of these policymakers, my staff and I were able to commit ourselves to using innovative strategies for attracting, training, and retaining the best available teachers—as well as principals and support staff. Here are some of the steps we implemented in Cherokee County.

Recruiting

Cherokee County's talent search for great teachers begins early in the year preceding their arrival in our district. Colleges and universities with highly respected programs for teacher preparation are frequent stops for personnel department staff and principals as they recruit. The school district empowers recruiters with the option of offering intent-to-hire contracts, which gives them an advantage in signing qualified candidates immediately.

Technology is also a valuable tool for recruiting teachers from diverse locations. For example, last year the district hired a teacher from Canada who had visited our Web site and interviewed through teleconferencing. Offering contracts to student teachers with outstanding performance in the classroom also gives us a head start on the competition.

Competitive Salaries and Benefits

Nearly one-half of teachers in the United States leave the profession within their first five years, typically citing low salaries and inadequate benefits as major reasons (Bolich, 2002). Because competitive salaries and an excellent fringe benefits package draw high-quality teachers and increase the pool of talent from which we select candidates, one of our top legislative priorities is to offer competitive salaries, and the district's board of education contributes a significant local supplement to enhance the state's standard salary. Our district also considers candidates' previous years of experience in its calculations of pay for veteran recruits. Teachers receive an increase of 10 percent on the state and local salaries when they have National Board Certification, an incentive that attracts teachers dedicated to improving their skills and craft.

In addition to competitive salaries, we offer a wellness benefit that includes payroll deductions for gym memberships and an employee assistance program that provides such benefits as 24-hour access to confidential counseling sessions for family, marital, emotional, financial, legal, or chemical dependency issues. We also offer a job-sharing program that allows individual teachers to work two and one-half days each week in tandem with another classroom teacher; 18 teachers participated during the 2002–2003 school year.

Summer Induction Program

With the teacher attrition rate in Georgia approaching 26 percent, we knew that preparing new teachers for the classroom and stemming the tide of teachers' departures required special action. We developed a comprehensive and inspiring program for teachers new to the district: the Camp Cherokee Summer Induction Program.

During two weeks in July, the Camp Cherokee program offers a menu of 32 informative workshops that span such crucial subjects as ethics, standards, technology, special education procedures, instructional strategies in reading and math, and using assessment data to improve student achievement. Through these opportunities, new hires experience both high-quality professional development and an introduction to the district's personnel, procedures, priorities, and curriculum standards. In one 2002 workshop, for example, the district's trained mentors, teachers of the year, and teachers certified by the National Board held grade-level panel discussions on discipline, instructional strategies, and system processes. The 2003 session offered publisher-directed training to all teachers on writing instruction, the new SAT assessments, and the newly adopted language arts textbooks. Compensation for participation in this voluntary program is a maximum of eight workshops and $1,600. Participants whose summer schedules allow attendance at fewer than eight workshops receive $200 for each workshop attended.

Camp Cherokee is a collaborative effort within the community and a phenomenal success. The district's professional development staff members work with local college or university professors, who serve as facilitators.

The program has an overall participant approval rating of 91 percent, and participants' evaluations indicate that the program has improved confidence and job satisfaction. In 2001, the district's overall retention rate for its 145 newly hired teachers was 95 percent, and 93 percent of the 280 new hires who attended Camp Cherokee in the summer of 2002 returned to our classrooms in the fall of 2003. As with most of the school district's initiatives, descriptions of Camp Cherokee courses are available on the district's Web site (www.cherokee.k12.ga.us/centralservices/professionaldevelopment/CampCherokeeBrochure.pdf).

Continuing Professional Development

In Cherokee County, employees can register and receive reimbursement for participating in online, job-embedded, standards-based, and collaborative professional development through several vendor providers. The district has also formed partnerships with several local colleges and universities—Reinhardt College, Piedmont College, Appalachian Technical College, and North Metro College—to enhance their preparation of teachers.

Through a partnership with Piedmont College, for example, employees can take courses toward master's degrees in early childhood education or secondary education in math, English, science, or social studies. These classes meet in classrooms and technology labs throughout the school system. This popular partnership allowed 21 of our employees to receive degrees, and 27 more employees are scheduled to finish in the spring of 2004.

Through a partnership with Appalachian Technical College, more than 100 of our paraprofessionals are taking courses to receive associate degrees and become early childhood specialists. This program serves to meet the paraprofessional requirements of the No Child Left Behind legislation. District teachers serve as instructors and model best education practices. Our first graduates are scheduled for 2005.

The district also provides financial and consultative support for teachers seeking National Board certification. So far, 17 teachers have attained National Board certification, and approximately 30 more are currently seeking this prestigious certification. As the number of teachers certified by the National Board grows, the resources available to new candidates also expand. Previously, the bulk of assistance to teachers came from Kennesaw State University's Teacher Center. Local teachers have now assumed responsibility for acting as mentors to candidates through a local candidate course, which supports teachers as they work on their portfolios and prepare for the test. In addition, Georgia now requires the Knowledgeable Teacher course for candidates who plan to seek reimbursement of fees from the state. Originally available only online, and limited in the number of candidates it could support, the course is now available in Cherokee County's 2003 summer course offerings through our professional development office. One of our school system's employees, who is certified by the National Board as a facilitator, will teach two sections of the course.

Additional financial incentives for teachers who take advanced course-work in content areas ensure that teachers will have subject-area knowledge that enhances their classroom teaching, not just coursework that qualifies them for job switches to guidance or administration. Any teacher who becomes certified in programs for the gifted or for English-language learners receives an additional stipend, thereby providing a fresh supply of competent instructors in these critical shortage areas. More than 400 teachers in the district have become certified in gifted education during the past two years, and 82 are certified instructors in English as a Second Language. To encourage continuity and experience in the classroom, substitute teachers who work 90 days during a regular school year receive an additional $500 stipend.

All of these financial incentives create better working conditions for teachers, tie our major system priorities to budgetary practices, and have a positive impact on teacher retention rates. Thanks to the district's zero-based budgetary process, which closely aligns expenditures with the system's major priorities, these programs are continuing in 2003–2004 despite the state's budget cuts.

Mentoring Program

Mentoring programs give teachers the support that they need early in their careers and reward mentors for sharing their experience and expertise with their colleagues. Cherokee County's Beginning Educator Support and Training (BEST) program offers special professional development aimed at the needs of the beginning teacher and strives to have a support system in place at the outset of a new teacher's career.

Principals choose teachers to work as mentors and in helpful partnerships according to grade level, subject matter, and physical proximity. The mentoring program handbook outlines the general requirements, such as weekly conferences during September and October and monthly conferences thereafter; written feedback and reflection by mentors of two classroom visits; and written feedback by protégés of observations of two classes taught by veteran teachers. New teachers use special notebooks to document their strategies for planning, teaching, and participating in school improvement activities that help integrate the new teacher into the school culture.

The professional development department maintains communication with mentors through biannual meetings, school visits, and quarterly newsletters.

Teachers may also take the Teacher Support Strategist course, a 100-hour, state-approved program for training mentors that includes 50 internship hours. Currently, mentors are not required to participate in this rigorous, yearlong training, but many have found it helpful and the financial incentive attractive.

Technology

Cherokee County has been a pioneer in providing the latest technological tools to classroom teachers, and our commitment to technology has provided an enticing and ongoing perk for our outstanding educators. Through the district's Laptops for Teachers Program and other initiatives, we have distributed more than 1,200 laptops to teachers who have completed the Georgia technology requirement for certification. By 2004, we expect that all 2,011 certified teachers will have received this state certification. Staff members from our departments of technology and professional development have created courses that integrate technology into the curriculum and improve teacher effectiveness through computer management.

All Cherokee teachers now use desktop computers to take attendance each period, enter and submit grades electronically, and provide information for parents, who can log on to the Internet and check the progress of their children each week and keep up with assignments. The district delivered more than 30,000 hours of technology training during the 2001–2002 school year.

Other initiatives—such as the use of personal digital assistants, student laptops, and mobile wireless labs in the classroom—attract teachers who possess the computer skills to teach students to become lifelong learners in the information age. We agree with the MetLife Foundation's recent report (2002), which asserts that the ability of a teacher to design instruction that prepares students for our technologically rich world is the characteristic of an excellent teacher. Because we are constantly updating our software and implementing new programs to enhance teaching and learning, we offer technology courses throughout the year to provide teachers with quick refreshers and to update their computer skills.

Among the new programs implemented this year is a user-friendly gradebook application that allows teachers to easily share students' grades and assignment information with parents through a special module. In addition, we have enhanced our e-mailing capabilities, the ease of scheduling facilities, and teachers' and students' access to instructional resources.

Teacher Recognition

According to Ingersoll (2001), teachers who leave the profession because of job dissatisfaction typically cite the lack of support from school administration; the lack of student motivation and discipline; and the lack of teacher influence over decision making. To increase the venues available for teachers to resolve issues that contribute to teacher turnover, I meet regularly with committees of teachers, and every school advisory council includes a teacher representative. I also meet several times with the teachers of the year from all of our schools to discuss important issues of concern. Many excellent ideas and suggestions come from these meetings. The district holds awards banquets for teachers of the year, recipients of the district's technology trailblazer awards, and teachers whose achievements and work on behalf of students have received recognition outside the district.

The Ongoing Challenge

Attracting and retaining the best teachers is imperative for developing a high-quality school district. Entrusted with the education of more than 28,400 students, the Cherokee County school board, staff members, and I are committed to improving the recruitment and training of our educators, who work daily to make a positive difference in students' lives. Teachers' work in the classroom produces the student learning necessary for a district to achieve internationally competitive standards. We must help teachers maintain the enthusiasm and dedication that called them into teaching; increase and enhance their skills and training; and value their voice and commitment. This ongoing challenge is one of our most important responsibilities.

References

Bolich, A. (2002). *Reduce your losses: Help new teachers become veteran teachers.* Atlanta, GA: Southern Regional Education Board.

Ingersoll, R. (2001). Teacher turnover and teacher shortages. *American Educational Research Journal, 38*(3), 499–534.

Marx, G. (2000). *Ten trends: Educating children for a profoundly different future.* Arlington, VA: Educational Research Service.

Prince, C. (2002, August). Missing: Top staff in bottom schools. *The School Administrator, 7,* 6–14.

Teacher Network Policy Institute. (2002). *Ensuring teacher quality.* New York: MetLife Foundation.

Part IV

Supporting Good Teachers

15

Know Why, Know How, Know Whom

Stepping-Stones to Success for Second-Career Teachers

Gail A. Mayotte

Gail A. Mayotte is director of curriculum and testing at the Archdiocese of Boston Department of Education, 2200 Dorchester Ave., Dorchester, MA 02124. She can be reached by phone at (617) 298-6555 and by e-mail at sgmayotte@abcso.org.

In recent years, education policymakers have responded to the looming teacher shortage by focusing more attention on recruiting midcareer professionals into teaching. Despite their relative age and maturity, second-career teachers are novices when they enter the classroom. Like all new teachers, they need support and guidance to build their confidence and strengthen their skills (Freidus, 1994; Madfes, 1990).

Yet individuals who enter teaching as a second career also have experiences, qualities, strengths, and concerns that differ from those of first-career teachers (Freidus, 1994; Novak & Knowles, 1992; Serow, 1993). For example, research has found that career switchers have a highly developed sense of mission, commitment, and professionalism that inspired them to move into teaching (Bullough & Knowles, 1990; Freidus, 1994; Haipt, 1987/1988; Resta, Huling, & Rainwater, 2001). Other research suggests that through their former work experiences, career switchers have developed a well-defined sense of self, understanding of human behavior, and skill in interactions with people (Freidus, 1992, 1994; Freidus & Krasnow, 1991; Haipt, 1987/1988). Conversely, research also shows that some career switchers struggle in the transition to teaching because of their preconceived notions, attitudes, and expectations shaped by previous work experiences (Bullough & Knowles, 1990; Curley, 1990; Freidus, 1992, 1994).

The Stepping-Stones

How can schools build on the specific strengths of second-career teachers to ease their transition to teaching? A recent qualitative study that looked at career switchers' perceptions about their first year of teaching offers some insights to address this question (Mayotte, 2001).

For the study, four novice second-career teachers participated in a series of three to five interviews over an eight-month period, discussing how their previous careers influenced their beliefs about teaching and learning and shaped their classroom practice. The teachers were all female, but they differed in age and previous career. They included a former engineer, age 25; a former administrative assistant, age 28; a former small business owner who had also been a behavioral psychologist, age 49; and a former magazine editor who had also been a commodities broker, age 48.

In addition, 25 second-career graduates of a master's degree program in education, now in their first year of teaching, responded to a written survey. The survey respondents had previously worked in a variety of occupations, including personnel management, physical therapy, fund raising, education research, and after-school program management. Survey questions addressed their adaptation to the role of teacher, their teaching philosophy, the relationship of their teaching competencies to the competencies that they had developed in their other careers, and support structures that existed for new teachers.

The results of this study suggest that schools can provide stepping-stones for a successful transition to teaching by building on three kinds of knowledge that career switchers developed in their previous careers: *know-why, know-how,* and *know-whom* (Arthur, Inkson, & Pringle, 1999; Defillippi & Arthur, 1994). The *know-why* competencies include an individual's motivation, personal values, beliefs, and goals within a career. The *know-how* competencies include skills, abilities, routines, and occupation-related knowledge. The *know-whom* competencies are networks, mentoring relationships, and social contacts. Many competencies outlast an employment setting, becoming "a moving base onto which new competencies are grafted" (Arthur, Inkson, & Pringle, 1999, p. 124).

When career switchers move to teaching, they bring differing levels of know-why, know-how, and know-whom competencies to their new career. However, these strengths do not automatically make the transfer to teaching an easy one for career switchers (Freidus, 1992, 1994; Powell, 1996). To build stepping-stones to success for second-career teachers, schools need to become sensitive to the special needs of this group in each competency area.

Provide Opportunities to Communicate About Know-Why Competencies

I wanted to try to get people to live on a better plane and I knew that teachers had a great influence on me. I don't know of a better way to do that than being in a public high school. I think an English teacher is the person in the position to move students that way.

—Former magazine editor, age 48

The know-why competencies relate to an individual's career motivation. They also include personal values and beliefs and professional identification. Second-career teachers have usually engaged in some soul searching and personal reflection in making the decision to move to teaching, and they tend to be fairly articulate and comfortable communicating their motivations, beliefs, and desires. But schools need to build on this strength by giving them constructive opportunities to articulate their values, and supportive listeners who help them translate their motivations and beliefs into teaching and classroom practice.

Preconceived notions and expectations about teaching shaped by previous work experiences can have negative effects on teaching practice if they go unexplored. For example, some second-career teachers who worked with high-aptitude adults in their previous careers tend to overestimate students' developmental levels and move too quickly through new material. Others, who come from business settings in which efficiency was prized and money was readily available, struggle to adjust to the school setting with its vast needs and limited resources. By engaging in guided and reflective inquiry, second-career teachers can examine their assumptions and make the necessary adjustments to new experiences.

Effective communication between second-career teachers and the personnel supporting them is essential. Opportunities for meaningful exchanges can help novice career switchers understand the influence of their personal values and beliefs on their teaching practice and help them articulate the personal meaning that they attach to their teaching career.

Give Consideration to Know-How Competencies

Having dealt with credit, I was able to bring that experience to help the students in 8th grade social studies understand why people used credit and why that was such a problem at the start of the Great Depression. I don't think that I would have taken that approach if I hadn't had a business background. In fact, I am hoping to teach an elective on personal finance. My business career is definitely coming into my teaching.

—Former business professional, age 40

The know-how competencies are the skills, abilities, routines, and occupation-related knowledge that an individual develops and accrues. Arthur and colleagues (1999) identify many *boundaryless benefits* that individuals develop in one career and can easily transfer to another. The surveyed second-career teachers recognized interpersonal skills, understanding of children and child development, managerial skills, and content knowledge as some of the boundaryless benefits that they developed in their first careers and could transfer to teaching. For example, one teacher believed that his experience as a grant writer and news reporter helped him teach writing skills. A former dental assistant and medical researcher noted that her experience in the medical field allowed her to share real-life examples and knowledge of situations that her biology students might face in their lives. A former engineer acknowledged that her previous career providing technical support for a software company had developed her extensive technological knowledge, which she passed on to her students.

Nonetheless, we cannot assume that competencies from former careers will easily transfer to teaching. Career switchers need support to adapt their prior knowledge and skills for the classroom. They need opportunities to consider how they can use their previously developed competencies within their teaching.

Career switchers in the study readily acknowledged that they desired and needed support regarding practical matters—strategies for conducting parent meetings, methods of completing report cards, curriculum guidance, and ideas about how to teach specific lessons. But they did not appreciate it when their schools ignored their previous career skills and life experience. For example, some of the career switchers were required to participate in novice teacher input sessions or courses that covered competencies that they had already developed through their experience. One second-career teacher indicated that in her school's teacher induction activities, "The types of things they focus on are classroom management, and I worked as a behavioral psychologist for many years when I got out of college. I don't need somebody to tell me how to manage people or how to conduct a parent meeting. Now if they were going to give me curriculum guidelines . . ." Thus, in assessing career switchers' needs regarding teaching practice, support programs need to take into consideration the previously developed knowledge and skills that the new teachers bring to the classroom.

Provide Connections to Build Know-Whom Competencies

If I didn't have that ability to reach out to other people, I can't imagine how I would have dealt with the stresses. . . . After I started getting support from Cathy, that gave me the impetus to seek out support from other people. And you know, it is very, very difficult when you're new to know where you can look for help. Everyone has got their own little thing going on, and unless somebody pokes their head in and says, "How are you doing?" it's really hard to figure out who might be open to your approaching them.

—Former business owner, age 49

The know-whom competencies include networks, mentoring relationships, and social contacts. Social and supportive connections are vital during the first years of teaching. School districts can help facilitate these connections by providing systematic induction programs that bring novice teachers together for informational and social exchanges, as well as matching new teachers with mentors for additional support.

Know-whom competencies are less likely than other competencies to transfer from the career switchers' previous occupations to their new teaching careers; thus, second-career teachers' needs in this area are similar to those of first-career novice teachers. Unfortunately, career switchers may be less likely to receive strong support: Because of their age and maturity, teachers, students, parents, colleagues, and even principals do not always perceive them as novices. Although, as one career switcher noted, "this may be flattering," it also may reduce the assistance that they receive in forming new connections. A second issue is potential awkwardness between the novice and his or her assigned mentor if the latter is substantially younger. One career switcher noted, "my mentor is the age of the kid I first babysat."

A third concern is that midcareer novice teachers may have more outside commitments than the average new teacher, hindering opportunities to make connections. One career switcher noted that responsibility for her children limited her participation in after-school events and social gatherings with fellow teachers. Another noted that the illness and subsequent death of her elderly mother limited some of her interactions with colleagues early in the academic year. Schools need to be aware of the specific circumstances of the individual second-career teacher to help that person adapt.

The age of career switchers can also influence the support they need. Research has shown that concerns within teaching may differ between younger and older beginning teachers (Bendixen-Noe & Redick, 1995). The older career switchers bring to teaching a longer history of personal and professional experiences that influence their beliefs, motivations, and new learning, as well as their needs.

Career switchers in the survey who had mentors consistently reported higher levels of satisfaction with the support that they received from their schools. Providing mentors and opportunities for peers to support one another, through support groups or Internet user groups, for example, allows novice career switchers to make connections and develop their know-whom competencies in the new environment of teaching.

Addressing the Needs of Career Switchers

The transition to the first year of teaching is challenging for any newcomer. Responses to this study illustrate that second-career teachers face many of the same challenges that their first-career colleagues do, but they also bring specific strengths and needs to their new profession. To best prepare career switchers for their work in teaching, schools need to put support structures in place that address the unique needs of these new teachers. Ideas for helpful practices include sensitivity to the outside commitments of career switchers, flexibility in mentor pairings, training of mentors to make them aware of the specific needs of older novice teachers, and the availability of peer support groups for second-career teachers.

All of these ideas require interaction. Opportunities to gather with colleagues may be the single most effective support structure for second-career teachers. Such opportunities provide a vehicle for communication to strengthen participants' personal sense of identity and meaning in the profession (the know-why competencies), create opportunities for consideration of practice (the know-how competencies), and afford a means to make connections (the know-whom competencies). By ensuring that these stepping-stones are in place, schools can help second-career teachers succeed.

References

Arthur, M., Inkson, K., & Pringle, J. (1999). *The new careers: Individual action and economic change.* Thousand Oaks, CA: Sage.

Bendixen-Noe, M., & Redick, S. (1995). Teacher development theory: A comparison between traditional-aged and nontraditional-aged beginning secondary teachers. *Action in Teacher Education, 17*(1), 52–59.

Bullough, R. V., Jr., & Knowles, J. G. (1990). Becoming a teacher: Struggles of a second-career beginning teacher. *International Journal of Qualitative Studies in Education, 3*(2), 101–112.

Curley, R. (1990). An innovative path to teaching: The view from education. In B. Risacher (Ed.), *Scientists and mathematicians become school teachers* (pp. 71–80). New York: National Executive Service Corps.

Defillippi, R., & Arthur, M. (1994). The boundaryless career: A competency-based perspective. *Journal of Organizational Behavior, 15,* 307–324.

Freidus, H. (1992). *Men in a woman's world: A study of male second-career teachers in elementary schools.* Paper presented at the annual meeting of the American Educational Research Association, San Francisco, CA.

Freidus, H. (1994). *Supervision of second-career teachers: What's our line?* Paper presented at the annual meeting of the American Educational Research Association, New Orleans, LA.

Freidus, H., & Krasnow, M. (1991). *Second-career teachers: Themes and variations.* Paper presented at the annual meeting of the American Educational Research Association, Chicago, IL.

Haipt, M. (1987/1988). Choosing teaching as a midcareer change. *The Teacher Educator, 23*(3), 17–24.

Madfes, T. J. (1990). Second career, second challenge: What do career changes say about the work of teaching? In B. Risacher (Ed.), *Scientists and mathematicians become school teachers* (pp. 25–33). New York: National Executive Service Corps.

Mayotte, G. (2001). *Examining the perceptions of second-career teachers regarding their first-year teaching experiences.* Unpublished doctoral dissertation, Boston College, Chestnut Hill, MA.

Novak, D., & Knowles, G. J. (1992). *Life histories and the transition to teaching as a second career.* Paper presented at the annual meeting of the American Educational Research Association, San Francisco, CA.

Powell, R. R. (1996). Teaching alike: A cross-case analysis of first-career and second-career beginning teachers' instructional convergence. *Teaching & Teacher Education, 13*(3), 341–355.

Resta, V., Huling, L., & Rainwater, N. (2001). Preparing second-career teachers. *Educational Leadership, 58*(8), 60–63.

Serow, R. C. (1993). Why teach? Altruism and career choice among nontraditional recruits to teaching. *Journal of Research and Development in Education, 26*(4), 197–204.

16

What Graduate Teacher Candidates Want

Mary Ann Smorra

Mary Ann Smorra is a professor at the School of Education, Georgian Court College, 900 Lakewood Ave., Lakewood, NJ 08701. She can be reached via e-mail at smorram@georgian.edu.

Bill was a state trooper. While assisting a motorist on the parkway, he was hit from behind, and his injuries meant that he soon found himself at a desk job. Following months of intense physical therapy, Bill decided to pursue an alternative career—teaching. Why? As he explained, "Just like working in the police department, teaching will give me the opportunity to help others. Supporting and helping students to become confident members of society in our changing and sometimes confusing world is the challenge that I look forward to."

Idealistic—yes, but not the words of a recent college graduate. Instead, along with the other teacher candidates in his class, Bill is an older-than-average graduate student. In his 30s, Bill is married and has three children. Does he want to make a commitment to our children, our students? Absolutely.

The graduate students in our education program at Georgian Court College, a private liberal arts college in Lakewood, New Jersey, always inspire me. Their commitment to education is evident in their coursework, thesis projects, and the glowing reports that come from the school districts in which they teach. The kudos are not just for their skills, but also for the heart and spirit with which they teach their students.

As their professor, however, I worry about them. I worry that their idealism will falter, that the bureaucracy of factory-like school districts will weigh them down and stultify their creativity and passion. To find out more about how they view their future role as teachers, I surveyed 17 outstanding teacher candidates who had taken some of my courses.

The survey responses reflect an enthusiastic group of future educators. Being part of a cohort group has nourished their resolve, particularly for those who have not been students for years, much less at the graduate level. Through the years, I have taught students who were making transitions from such professions as lawyer, flight instructor, nuclear engineer, biologist, personal trainer, and interior decorator. Our program provides students with cohort support during their matriculation, student teaching, and first years of teaching. The bonds forged and friendships made in these cohorts help foster these teachers' commitment to their new profession.

The survey respondents were between 25 and 46 years old. Their undergraduate majors ranged from business to psychology, sociology to English, criminal justice to family studies. Their former career choices were equally diverse. All the students surveyed, however, have a common goal: to become excellent teachers who influence their students' lives in a positive way. To help sustain their energy and idealism, we should pay attention to their answers.

Why Do You Want to Become a Teacher?

The responses to this question were the most heartfelt. Having already experienced other professions, students were aware of why they wanted to become teachers. Lisa, for example, said, "After graduation from college, I entered the business world and worked as a recruiter. Although the job was financially rewarding, I felt no sense of accomplishment or pride. A career in teaching will provide me with a deeper sense of purpose and pride in my work."

What Are the Qualities of a Good Teacher?

The teacher candidates noted such attributes as patience, creativity, trustworthiness, a sense of humor, a nurturing personality, good communication skills, a high level of organization, a commitment to the success of students, and a sensitivity to students' needs and feelings. As Stacey commented,

Good teachers are in touch with their students and enjoy a high level of respect. Good teachers are up on current methods in education and use a variety of methods to benefit every learner. Good teachers have an excellent rapport with parents and other teachers. Good teachers challenge students to high levels of success and allow students to be individuals.

Stephen simply replied, "A good teacher is a good listener." And many described the good teacher as a learner.

What Conditions Do You Need for Job Satisfaction?

Three key conditions were most important to these survey respondents: being able to teach students successfully (75 percent); having the support of the school community (44 percent); and receiving fair pay (31 percent). Other important conditions that they felt would create a sense of fulfillment were to learn on the job; to experience success in life; and to feel good about oneself. Elissa expressed her resolve: "No matter what the district or budget or expensive gadgets or the lack thereof, I want to teach, and a good teacher will find a way to do that with or without the bells and whistles."

Robyn echoed this idealism: "I would want more than anything to instill a love of learning in my students. I want my students to learn in an environment where they feel confident to be who they are."

These teacher candidates also said that they want to develop a healthy rapport with administrators, colleagues, and parents. They want the support of these groups and opportunities for staff development and professional growth. Tony was optimistic: "I believe that I will become part of a strong and devoted community that has the best interests of students as its goal. I expect to come home each day believing that I have made a difference in a student's life."

These teacher candidates placed finances in a realistic framework. They did not expect huge compensation packages, but they wanted fair pay. Sarah's perspective was typical: "I expect to enjoy my work, especially inside the classroom. I want to be respected by my coworkers and administrators. I would feel fulfilled if there were job promotions, too."

A realistic response came from Bill: "If I expect certain conditions to be met, then I am setting myself up for disappointment. The only condition that must be met is one that I place on myself: to have a positive attitude."

Why Do Schools Lose Good Teachers?

These teacher candidates' perceptions of why teachers leave the education profession are revealing. The two reasons most frequently given correspond to two of the expectations: low salary (63 percent), and lack of support from the administration, the community, or parents (63 percent).

Regarding salary, Tony was pragmatic: "Salary is probably the leading cause of why education loses good teachers. When you look at the time that we have invested both in and out of class, you can understand why some people leave the profession. If you are looking at achieving a good hourly salary, though, teaching is not the profession to be in."

Lack of support was a strong concern among the teacher candidates. Kim elaborated on how teachers can support one another:

> Teachers sometimes feel isolated. They are always in their classrooms and are not able to share ideas and have plain old conversations as most adults do in other work environments. Teachers should reach out to other teachers and share ideas and thoughts on their teaching. They would learn a lot from one another. I am sure that they could share solutions and ideas on all kinds of ways to deal with lessons, students, and parents.

These teacher candidates are ripe for education's recent emphasis on creating classroom and professional school communities.

The Challenge

In the schools in which I have taught, administered, and supervised, the environments that have been most conducive to professional and personal growth correspond with what these teacher candidates say that they most need and want. Their comments remind us of the care and mentoring that are so crucial for keeping new teachers in education. We must find ways to nurture the compassion and excellence of those who join our profession.

17

Four Ways to Sustain All Teachers

Kathleen Webbert Glaser

Kathleen Webbert Glaser, a former school principal, is an educational consultant and an instructor in educational studies at St. Mary's College of Maryland, P.O. Box 1, St. Mary's City, MD 20686. She can be reached via e-mail at kwglaser@smcm.edu.

I became a school leader because I wanted to support teachers who are committed to making a positive difference in students' lives. For 19 years, I served as principal at Hollywood Elementary School, a K–5 public school in St. Mary's County, Maryland. As a school leader, I continually asked myself, "What conditions must a principal provide to sustain good teachers?" To answer this question, I implemented four strategies to help support teachers both professionally and personally. Any school can adapt the following practices to achieve excellent results:

- Build a positive school culture that supports teaching and learning.
- Provide differentiated professional development opportunities.
- Institute family-friendly policies in the workplace.
- Encourage teacher innovation.

These strategies allow teachers not only to teach, but also to learn, collaborate, and innovate—activities that are key to teacher morale and job satisfaction.

A Positive School Culture

Barth aptly describes school culture as "the historically transmitted pattern of meaning that wields astonishing power in shaping what people think and how they act" (2002, p. 7). He identifies the role of the principal as "culture builder," a definition that matches my experience. The quality of a school's ethos—its shared beliefs, traditions, values, and attitudes—is key to making the school a place in which students and faculty can thrive as a community of learners and leaders.

When a principal makes student learning central to the school's daily operation, teachers are inspired to be there day after day and year after year, focusing on their students' learning and improving their own pedagogical skills and knowledge. Creating opportunities for dialogue and collaboration among teachers was central to my school's success as an education community and enabled teachers to share with colleagues the complex challenges and joys of their important work.

At our school, we built a positive culture through teacher conferences, faculty meetings, and hiring decisions. Our focus was on allowing teachers to teach according to their strengths, which enabled us to reach a broad cross-section of learners, and to use diverse teaching approaches and multiple solutions to classroom challenges. Some teachers conducted arts-infused social studies programs; others led outdoor science investigations that resulted in student-written proposals for on-site ecology projects. We shared relevant research on such topics as brain-based learning and multiple intelligences to confirm our collective experience that one size does not fit all—for our students or for us. Such a diversity-friendly environment relieves teachers of the pressure to become carbon copies of an idealized model teacher, and each teacher's special gifts can enhance the rich mix of school offerings for students.

A high rate of staff retention and positive teacher comments demonstrated the success of our school's philosophy. One teacher noted, "I would have left teaching if I hadn't experienced the climate of acceptance here that made me believe in my own gifts as a teacher and know that the reasons I went into teaching are valued."

Differentiated Professional Development

When I reflect on my own reasons for being drawn to education as a career, the sense of discovery inherent in a dynamic learning environment is near the top of my list. Because our school's well-designed staff development program produced varying degrees of teacher learning and response, we pursued funding sources to enabe teachers to attend professional conferences, visit exemplary classrooms and programs, and share their own expertise with their peers. We also began inviting teachers to join administrators for other professional development experiences. Traveling together to conferences or to observe school programs provided optimal conditions to share with one another our observations, insights, and plans.

The results of these joint learning excursions were far-reaching. For example, attending arts-in-education workshops at the Kennedy Center in Washington, D.C., initiated a tradition of arts residencies at Hollywood Elementary. These one-week programs bring artists, poets, musicians, and dancers into the school, where they work with four to five classes on various arts projects and performances. The team of teachers that coordinates these residencies participates annually in Maryland's Teacher/Artist Summer Institute, which is cosponsored by the Maryland State Department of Education and the Maryland State Arts Council. During this summer program, artists conduct workshops to demonstrate strategies for infusing the arts across the curriculum. Each school team creates an action plan for implementing these strategies and arranging arts residencies for its school community.

Another special professional development opportunity coincided with our planning for a new school building designed to facilitate teacher collaboration and project learning. We attended a mini-conference in Orlando on "The New Elementary School" that featured Lilian Katz, whose writings had influenced the development of our school's innovative, multi-age primary program. A team of four of us flew to Orlando—subsidized by personal as well as school funds—and had productive discussions with Lilian Katz and her associate, Sylvia Chard. Sylvia Chard later came to our new school to conduct an inservice program for our new staff at the beginning of the school year. Her project approach—teaching strategies that enable teachers to guide students through in-depth studies of real-world topics—permeated our classrooms and resulted in impressive student investigations and products.

The teachers at Hollywood know that the school administration considers as a priority their requests for training in such areas as technology, autism, environmental education, and multiple intelligences—essentially any subject directly linked to their assessment of student needs—and funds those requests as much as possible. The recognition of teachers' need to expand their professional knowledge is a powerful tool in keeping teachers engaged and energized.

Family-Friendly Policies

Family-friendly policies reduce teacher attrition by relieving the tension that many teachers feel when they try to balance the duties of being both responsible parents and dedicated teachers. In addition to allowing school staff to flex their schedules whenever possible, Hollywood Elementary developed job sharing as a viable option for teachers who needed more time to meet their family's needs. During the past 10 years, seven different pairs of teaching partners cotaught classes as a means to continue working in the profession while also devoting time to their own children. When my youngest child was born, I was working with a superintendent who permitted me to work a four-day week at a reduced salary for a year; this experience made me realize that time can be a more important factor than salary for working parents. When teachers feel good about meeting their personal responsibilities as parents, they teach more productively.

Rachel, an experienced teacher who had been juggling her responsibilities as a mother of three with her professional commitments, sought the option of job sharing for two years. Today, once more a full-time teacher, she looks back at her experience as "a great way to renew myself personally and professionally." As a bonus, she found that working so closely with a colleague allowed her to learn more about herself as a teacher, in addition to enjoying the "synergy of two teachers working together."

Of course, coteaching a class requires careful coordination and both teachers' firm commitment to daily communication. This thoughtful coordination maximizes the benefits that students receive from the strengths and insights of two teachers instead of one.

Another family-friendly school policy that teachers appreciated was the option to flex their regular work hours when family or personal needs required them to be away from their classrooms for a few hours. This policy allowed them to fulfill personal needs without having to take off an entire day and have a substitute teach their class. Hollywood also supports and encourages teachers' needs to participate in conferences and special events at their own children's schools.

Teacher Innovation

Thoughtful teacher innovation within the schoolhouse makes good use of the wisdom of experienced educators. Cara is an award-winning teacher who was widely recognized in our school community for designing a classroom environment and instructional program in which all students—including gifted students and those with special needs or behavioral issues—make significant progress. During her years in the profession, Cara sometimes heard the unspoken message that successful educators become administrators. But she was not interested in becoming a principal or supervisor. Certainly there should be a vital, innovative role in our schools for career teachers like Cara, for those who possess a depth and breadth of professional knowledge that would be a great benefit for any school.

What sustains teachers like Cara? "It's the opportunity to innovate as a classroom teacher and to create a successful learning environment for students that makes it all worthwhile," she says. "When you feel valued and respected as a professional and empowered to make the decisions you deem necessary for your students, you feel more invested in your teaching and good about your choice to be a teacher." Her innovations included organizing and teaching a multi-age class for students in grades 1–3, which met the needs of several primary students who performed better in a multi-age environment than in single-grade classrooms and benefited from learning under the same teacher for three years.

Supporting the innovations proposed by good teachers is key, not only to keeping those teachers in the classroom, but also to creating a self-renewing school. Hollywood Elementary received local, state, and national recognition for numerous teacher-led innovations, including multi-age classrooms, project-based learning, launching a community recycling program, and using the environment as an integrating context for interdisciplinary learning (Lieberman & Hoody, 1998).

My father-in-law, a retired chemist, supervised a research and development lab and studied the optimal lab conditions for fostering results-oriented, successful innovations. He developed the "Glaser Innovation Index," an assessment instrument that identifies seven crucial elements of the innovation process (Glaser, 1976). One element dictates that each research chemist needs a "champion" at the higher level of the organization to regularly discuss the questions, obstacles, and problems that the chemist confronts in his or her daily pursuit of the innovation or solution. The role of the champion in a research lab mirrors the role of the principal in supporting teacher innovation in the classroom. As a colleague who listens, and as a champion who is invested in the teacher's problem-solving process, the principal creates conditions within the schoolhouse for shared instructional leadership and successful innovation that benefit students and sustain teachers.

The Solution

Good teachers are our strongest resource, and only by enhancing and tapping into that resource can we create successful learning communities. One colleague in Virginia asked the principal of her child's school, "What have you done in the past year to nurture and inspire the teachers in your school?" This question may seem unusual juxtaposed with today's seemingly omnipresent question: "How are your school's test scores?" But now is the time for serious contemplation of how we sustain our teachers. In *The Courage to Teach*, Parker Palmer raises similarly penetrating questions: "Many of us became teachers for reasons of the heart, animated by a passion for some subject and for helping people learn. But many of us lose heart as the years of teaching go by. How can we take heart in teaching once more so that we can, as good teachers always do, give heart to our students?" (1998, p. 17)

References

Barth, R. S. (2002). The culture builder. *Educational Leadership, 59*(8), 6–11.

Glaser, M. A. (1976). The innovation index. *Chemtech, 6,* 182.

Lieberman, G. A., & Hoody, L. L. (1998). *Closing the achievement gap using the environment as an integrating context for learning* (pp. 85–87). Poway, CA: Science Wizards.

Palmer, P. J. (1998). *The courage to teach.* San Francisco: Jossey-Bass.

Four Ways to Support Special Educators

Cheryl Fielding and Cindy Simpson

Cheryl Fielding is the coordinator of the Educational Diagnostician Program at the University of Texas-Pan American. She can be reached by phone at (956) 381-3404 or by e-mail at fieldingc@panam.edu. Cindy Simpson is assistant professor of education at Sam Houston State University in the Department of Language, Literacy, and Special Populations. She can be reached by phone at (936) 294-4045 or by e-mail at cindysimp@aol.com.

Special educators enter the field knowing that they will face the challenge of making a positive difference in the lives of students whose needs can differ dramatically from those of typically developing students. Even so, these professionals may become overwhelmed when they encounter the reality of diverse student needs and the demands of constantly changing laws, regulations, and expectations.

The current special education system in the United States evolved from the 1975 Public Law 94-142 (now known as the Individuals with Disabilities Education Act), which for the first time guaranteed a "free, appropriate public education" to every student, including those with disabilities. During the law's 28-year history, the categories of students qualifying for special education services have been refined and the numbers of students receiving these services have grown steadily. Public schools now provide special education services to about 6 million students (about 12 percent of all students ages 6–17) who fall into 13 disability categories: specific learning disabilities, speech or language impairments, mental retardation, emotional disturbance, multiple disabilities, hearing impairments, orthopedic impairments, other health impairments, visual impairments, autism, deafness or blindness, traumatic brain injury, and developmental delay (U. S. Department of Education, 2002).

Public expectations for the services provided by special educators have also evolved during the past few decades. For example, interpretations of the federal law's requirement that students with disabilities be educated with their nondisabled peers to the "maximum extent appropriate" and in the "least restrictive environment possible" (Individuals with Disabilities Act, 20 U.S.C. § 1412, 1997 have changed. Common school practices have moved from providing special education services in separate classrooms, to pulling students out for help in resource rooms, to mainstreaming students with disabilities with their peers for parts of the day. Today, many school policymakers and courts interpret the law to require inclusion—adapting regular classroom instruction so that it meets the individual needs of all students, including those with disabilities (*Education Week*, 2002).

A Daunting Challenge

The increasing number of students in special education, and the changing context in which schools serve these students, makes recruiting highly qualified special education teachers more important than ever. But attracting and retaining special educators is a daunting challenge. Research has documented shortages of both special education teachers (Lemke & Harrison, 2000) and related service and assessment personnel (Hausman & Hausman, 1999; Simpson, 2002). And the shortages appear to be growing.

In the past 20 years, there has been a 30 percent decrease in the number of doctorates awarded in special education, and the shortage of minority special education teachers is even more acute (Educational Testing Service, 2003).

These shortages are at least partly the result of a system that overwhelms those who enter the special education profession (Shure, 2001). The Council for Exceptional Children noted that teaching conditions in special education had pushed the field into crisis (Kozleski, Mainzer, & Deshler, 1998). The report attributed this crisis to six major problems within the system:

1. Unqualified individuals teaching students with disabilities.
2. Overwhelming paperwork.
3. Insufficient time for individualized instruction.

4. Insufficient time for collaboration.

5. High caseloads.

6. Inadequate administrative and district support.

Fortunately, some school administrators have taken these concerns to heart and have implemented creative but practical approaches to attract and retain special education personnel. The Council for Exceptional Children's report and input from state agencies, professional associations, educators, and the community can be helpful in developing such innovative approaches. By using innovative strategies, such as the four that we suggest here, school leaders can counteract the special education system's problems and support special education teachers.

Provide Ongoing Professional Development

Good professional development enables teachers to continually become better at their jobs, which benefits schools and students. It also bolsters morale and is often key to teacher retention.

Dade County Public Schools in Florida faced the common problems of an inadequate supply of new special education teachers and burnout among its existing special education staff. To address these problems, Ron Felton, assistant superintendent of Dade County Schools, encouraged area universities to collaborate to offer a graduate degree in autism. He then offered teachers who worked with students with autism in his district the chance to earn this degree, paid for by the school system. Ron also recruited people from the local community with bachelor's degrees in psychology or social work to become special education teachers and to earn graduate degrees in special education, again paid for by the school system. Almost all of these individuals have remained with the district and now thrive in their new capacity (Council for Exceptional Children, 2002).

School systems that have fewer resources can creatively and cost-effectively provide professional development for teachers by using such state of-the-art technology as video teleconferencing equipment. For example, special education assessment personnel from the Dallas Independent School District recently viewed the evaluation of a child with autism at the University of Texas-Pan American, more than 600 miles away. Participants at the Dallas location interacted with the examiner and the child's parent during the evaluation. The use of the video teleconferencing equipment was provided by a grant from the Autism Treatment Center of Dallas. This type of professional development activity gives staff members access to the specialized expertise of professionals that may otherwise be beyond their reach because of travel expenses and scheduling conflicts.

Reduce the Paperwork Burden

Several education leaders have taken innovative approaches to reducing the burden of paperwork and administrative tasks that can often overwhelm special educators and keep them from the important job of serving students. Two such approaches involve reassigning such tasks to school assistant principals and hiring paraprofessional special education clerks.

Berty Rodriguez began her career as a special education teacher but later entered administration. As an assistant principal in Brownsville, Texas, she took responsibility for completing all of the multidisciplinary paperwork required at special education team meetings, an unprecedented step. Multidisciplinary paperwork can be more than 25 pages per meeting. It includes all aspects of a student's individualized education program as mandated by state and federal laws. This lengthy paperwork is typically completed by special education teachers during their conference or lunch periods or before school, or by educational diagnosticians who have a multitude of other evaluation duties. By assuming this duty, Berty removed the burden of paperwork from the special education teachers and educational diagnosticians in her school, and the process gave her a greater sense of ownership in the special education process.

Berty later became the special education director for Los Fresnos Independent School District, a neighboring district in southern Texas. Here, with the support of the superintendent, she made changes in the district's entire special education program on the basis of the lessons she had learned in Brownsville.

As Berty reviewed the district's special education paperwork she realized that many of the forms were difficult to understand because they included complex legal language. Further, school personnel received these forms in no specific order. Berty revised the district's special education forms so that they are now presented in a sensible and reasonable sequence. At the beginning of each school year, she spends one half-day updating school administrators on the correct methods for completing multidisciplinary team paperwork. Administrators report that once they receive this training, they feel comfortable with the process.

Special education training is crucial for all administrators and general education faculty. Each needs to have an understanding of the importance of the special education multidisciplinary team process and its valuable purpose in serving students with disabilities.

Berty believes that having assistant principals trained and responsible for multidisciplinary team paperwork makes sense for several reasons. It reduces high caseload and paperwork demands on teachers and educational diagnosticians, thus providing them with more time for instruction and collaboration. Special education personnel report that they feel supported and experience a greater sense of success with students. Administrators claim that they feel more involved in the lives of students with disabilities and their families, and that they can now field procedural questions without having to refer to specialists. Educational diagnosticians have more time to engage in collaborative efforts in such areas as in-home training for parents and assistive technology. Finally, Berty reports that this procedure has enabled the district to stay within the mandated timelines for evaluations.

The principal of a large middle school in northern Texas took a different approach to the paperwork problem. The school's special educators felt overburdened by scheduling and coordinating multidisciplinary team meetings. When meetings had to be postponed and rescheduled, stress levels rose because of such legal time constraints as the requirement to hold multidisciplinary team meetings within 30 calendar days of the full individual evaluation. The special education teachers also had to perform administrative duties in connection with these meetings—for example, completing and mailing notices for the meetings and keeping logs ensuring that the required procedural safeguard forms had been sent to parents. These tasks all cut into the teachers' lunch and planning periods.

In response to these concerns, the school principal assigned a paraprofessional who had training in scheduling, preparation of multidisciplinary meeting notices, and record keeping to work with the special education teachers on these basic clerical activities. Later, the paraprofessional took on the additional responsibility of assisting the special education teachers and assessment personnel with other organizational tasks, such as managing students' special education records. After the paraprofessional assumed these responsibilities, teachers' morale improved. The reduced paperwork demands made their jobs less stressful and enabled them to spend more time providing instruction and collaborating with one another.

The entire district subsequently adopted this innovative approach and has created new, permanent positions for paraprofessional special education clerks. District personnel administrators report that having these clerks gives them an edge over other districts when recruiting new special education teachers.

Reduce Class Size and Caseloads

As noted earlier, policymakers have identified high caseloads and large class sizes as major problems within the special education system. Some states have addressed the problem of large caseloads by setting reasonable statewide limits. For example, the Oklahoma State Department of Education establishes caseload and class-size requirements on the basis of full-time equivalents for special education (Oklahoma State Department of Education, 2002). Special education classes may have no more than 10 students at any time, unless the department's Special Education Services office grants special permission to adjust class size. If special educators also work with students in the general education environment, the department uses a formula to determine the teacher's maximum caseload on the basis of the percentage of time students spend in special or general education classes. The state put a similar formula in place for special education-related service personnel, such as speech-language pathologists.

In states that have no mandated caseload or class-size limits, professionals must rely on such organizations as the Texas Educational Diagnosticians' Association, the Council for Exceptional Children, and the National Association of School Psychologists for best-practice guidelines. A statewide survey of special education assessment specialists in Texas revealed that 68 percent of the 874 respondents had caseloads between 76 and 175 (Fielding, 2002a). This kind of study can provide guidelines for professionals to use in determining what constitutes an appropriate and manageable caseload.

One educational diagnostician in Texas reported using survey data to effect changes in caseload size and salary in her district. When she learned that the caseload sizes carried in her district were almost twice that of the state average and that the average salaries of educational diagnosticians in her district were more than $5,000 below the state average, she used this information to approach the special education director and request salary and caseload size adjustments. The district subsequently funded additional positions to reduce caseload sizes and granted stipends on the basis of the advanced degree required for the position of educational diagnostician (Fielding, 2002b).

Bring Diversity into the Field

The shortage of special education teachers is especially acute for racial and ethnic minority teachers. Whitworth (2000) notes that special education teachers must be able to teach students from linguistically and culturally diverse backgrounds. Minority students make up a significant proportion of the students in special education; in fact, their overrepresentation in certain categories of special education is a long-standing problem (Losen & Orfield, 2002). The Bank Street College points to "an urgent need to address the under-representation of African American and Hispanic special education teachers relative to the minority student population in special education classes. Minority teachers serve as role models for minority children and youth, and enrich the school and community with their personal knowledge of both the heritage and the issues facing culturally and linguistically diverse groups" (Usher, n.d.).

One successful effort to recruit diverse individuals to join the special education field was developed by Abilene Christian University and the Big Country Center for the Professional Development of Teachers. Using a grant from the Texas Board of Educator Certification, Abilene initiated Project PRIME (Preparing, Recruiting, and Retaining Teachers for Inclusive, Multicultural Environments).

In their recruitment efforts, Project PRIME staff members used several strategies to attract culturally diverse special educators. For example, they produced a professional video that highlighted the challenges and rewards of teaching in special education, and they developed a manual to assist university students in obtaining financial aid, which is often available to students who seek careers in special education.

Project PRIME staffers also held lunch meetings with local leaders of the African American and Latino communities to initiate a dialogue about ways to encourage minority high school students to pursue careers in special education.

To follow up on these meetings, Project PRIME staff members brought local minority high school students to the college campus and assisted them in the application and enrollment process. In addition, graduate students and faculty from Abilene visited high schools to share information about disability awareness and discuss special education as a career choice.

Jerry Whitworth, Chair of Abilene's Department of Education, suggests other innovative ideas for recruiting teachers from diverse populations (2000):

- Create a student ambassadorship program that brings university students majoring in special education to their former high schools to speak to prospective special educators.
- Develop scholarships and other incentives for students to select special education as a career option.
- Form a speakers bureau that includes special education teachers, support personnel, parents of children with disabilities, and representatives of various service providers to speak to high school and college students.
- Develop a media plan directed toward specific groups, such as bilingual individuals.
- Develop a program to assist minority teacher education candidates in the successful completion of required university program entrance and teacher certification examinations.

A Renewed System

Special educators face tough challenges and obstacles and need all the support that they can get. Just a few innovative ideas can help make systematic changes that will improve working conditions for special educators. By implementing some of the practical approaches presented here, administrators may soon see decreased staff turnover and increased retention of special education personnel.

These ideas help reduce caseloads and paperwork, provide more time for individualized instruction and professional collaboration, and help increase the number of qualified individuals teaching students with disabilities. Most important, by enabling special educators to do the work that they need to do with students, these approaches help to bring about higher levels of job satisfaction and retention. To improve education services for all students with disabilities, we must start with the teachers.

References

Council for Exceptional Children. (2002). Ron Felton: The superman of special education administrators. *CEC Today Online, 9*(4), 2. Available: www.cec.sped.org/bk/cec_today/nov_dec_2002/cectoday_11_2002_02.html

Education Week. (2002, November 1). *Inclusion* [Online]. Available: www.edweek.org/context/topics/issuespage.cfm?id=47

Educational Testing Service. (2003). *Congress to consider IDEA reauthorization* [Online]. Available: www.ets.org/textonly/regions/dco/newswash.htm/#congress

Fielding, C. (2002a). Statewide survey results: Part I of II. *The DiaLog, 31*(3), 8–12.

Fielding, C. (2002b). Statewide survey results: Part II of II. *TheDiaLog, 32*(1), 8–16.

Hausman, R., & Hausman, K. (1999, March). Use of selected available technology to provide relatively inexpensive distance learning courses along the Texas/Mexico "Border Corridor." In D. Montgomery (Ed.), *Rural special education for the new millennium.* Proceedings of the 19th Annual Conference of the American Council on Rural Special Education, Albuquerque, NM.

Individuals with Disabilities Education Act, 20 U.S.C. § 1400 *et seq.* (1997).

Kozleski, E., Mainzer, R., & Deshler, D. (1998). *Bright futures for exceptional learners: An action agenda to achieve quality conditions for teaching and learning.* Reston, VA: Council for Exceptional Children.

Lemke, J., & Harrison, S. (2000). Changing paradigms: A new teacher education model for rural Hawaii. *Rural Special Education Quarterly, 19*(3/4), 44–49.

Losen, D. J., & Orfield, G. (2002). *Racial inequity in special education.* Cambridge, MA: Harvard University Press.

Oklahoma State Department of Education. (2002). *Special Education Policies and Procedures Manual.* Oklahoma City, OK: Author. Available: www.sde.state.ok.us/pro/spedpp.html

Shure, J. (2001). Front and center. *Techniques: Connecting Education and Careers, 76*(3), 8.

Simpson, C. (2002). *Factors influencing the recruitment and retention of educational diagnosticians as perceived by special education directors in Texas.* Unpublished dissertation, Texas A&M University, College Station, TX.

U.S. Department of Education, Office of Special Education Services. (2002). *Twenty-third annual report to Congress on the Implementation of the Individuals with Disabilities Education Act.* Washington, DC: Author. Available: www.ed.gov/offices/OSERS/OSEP/Products/OSEP2001AnlRpt

Usher, A. (n.d.). Partnerships: Building routes to success for noncredentialed teachers in New York City public schools [Online]. Available: www.cec.sped.org/osep/database/detailView.html?masterID=577

Whitworth, J. (2000, March). *Preparing, recruiting, and retaining special education personnel in rural areas.* Paper presented at the meeting of the American Council on Rural Special Education, Alexandria, VA.

19

How Professional Dialogue Prevents Burnout

Grzegorz Mazurkiewicz

Grzegorz Mazurkiewicz is a social science teacher at a high school in Zabrze, Poland, and a project coordinator and consultant at the Center for Citizenship Education in Warsaw, Poland. He can be reached via e-mail at mazuranna@poczta.fm.

Teachers are constantly interacting with other people: students, parents, other teachers, experts, consultants, school administrators, school board members, representatives of local governments, and other school workers. But teachers are alone when they perform their most important task: educating young people.

Some argue that teachers have plenty of opportunities to talk with one another. Unfortunately, these discussions usually do not focus on supporting one another's teaching. Why do teachers talk about grades, individual students, school absences, the choice of a principal, or financial issues and not about how they teach and how best to educate students? The answer is that such conversations are very difficult. Teachers have not learned how to conduct such conversations, and nobody is helping them.

We need to have these conversations, however, to change the way we teach. Many believe that learning is the acquisition of accepted truths, but real learning occurs only when students construct meaning for themselves. Too often, we do not cultivate our students' natural curiosity or interest in learning (Costa, 2001). We need to help develop students' thinking skills instead of their memorization of facts. Changing our beliefs and habits, however, is difficult.

Launching a Critical Friends Group

At a high school in Zabrze, Poland, teachers at the first faculty meeting in the 2001–2002 school year heard an unusual offer: *Let's meet today after lessons to talk about our work. Throughout the year, we will meet once a month at someone's home to talk about how we teach in our classrooms. We will conduct each meeting according to a specific protocol, with one of us acting as moderator.*

Six teachers from different departments—including history, English, social science, physical education, and computer science—answered the invitation that day. At our first meeting, we spoke of our desire for constant learning, our fear of burning out, and our hope of conversing about our professional work. One said, "I want to fight the sense of isolation that is so common in this profession." Another said, "I would like to overcome the psychological barriers that I have to talking about my work." Still another wanted the answer to an important question: "Why am I teaching?"

We decided to devote our free time to this experiment because we knew that reflection about our work would require additional effort. We committed ourselves to the principles and procedures of Critical Friends, a protocol for professional conversation, mutual support, and critique that was developed in the United States by the Coalition of Essential Schools (Bambino, 2002).

The group started by establishing a few basic rules. Meetings would start on time and last no longer than two hours. We would hold meetings according to a previously accepted schedule and agree on topics in advance of the next meeting. A moderator would watch the time limits for speaking, designate the order of the speakers, and make sure that the discussion did not stray from the topic. We would start each meeting with short warm-up conversations on relatively light topics before discussing the main topic. We agreed to work on being open to others' ideas and to use nonthreatening "I statements" (such as "I think," "It seems to me") when we put forward opinions. Finally, all our conversations and actions would concentrate only on students and the school.

How well did we do? We never were able to start a meeting on time, but we did learn how to focus our conversations and how to help one another become better teachers. We learned how to plan our meetings to concentrate on professional improvement and discussions and analysis of our individual styles of work. Having one person who made up the schedule and a consistent moderator also helped our meetings run more smoothly. We managed to introduce an atmosphere of cooperation instead of competition. We developed an atmosphere of safety and trust during our carefully planned meetings, and we began to develop a better understanding of teaching and learning.

Opening Doors to Professional Dialogue

To prepare for each meeting, we read materials related to such discussion topics as engaging students in learning. We examined case studies, student work, and lesson scenarios. We discussed how to conduct observations of other classrooms and how to videotape lessons. We worked together on ways to improve our individual teaching strategies.

Observing Colleagues

We usually teach behind closed doors, with about 30 students in the classroom. The Critical Friends group decided to open up these doors by videotaping the introductory part of each group member's lesson. We wanted to see how we each organized the first 10 minutes of our lessons and sparked students' interest in our subjects. We called our project Colleague Observation.

Each member decided which class and lesson to record and show to the group. Another group member would help set up the video camera so that the teacher could easily turn it on for 10 minutes at the beginning of class. Later on in the year, we taped the last 10 minutes of each group member's class and analyzed how we gave our students instructions about their work.

To make the viewing of the lessons conducive to authentic reflection and help, the observing teachers concentrated on observing and analyzing what was going on in the classroom, and not on evaluating the teacher or the teacher's methods. Before watching the videos, for example, we agreed on the principles for starting a lesson well. While watching the video, participants asked themselves these questions:

- What do students understand?
- What questions are teachers asking?
- What questions are students asking?
- What is not clear for students?
- What would I do in such a situation?
- What else could be done to spark interest in the lesson?

These questions provided a useful way to concentrate on what was taking place in the classroom and to present new ideas without blaming or criticizing. As we watched the 10-minute videos, we each wrote down our questions and our most important observations on cards. After watching the videotape of a teacher's lesson, we talked about what we saw and what the teacher did to start or complete the lesson, comparing the teacher's actions with the principles we had set up beforehand. Our many differences of opinion made these discussions very lively, but we did develop a new set of principles for starting the lesson: introducing the subject and goal, engaging students in the topic, linking the new material with previous knowledge, asking interesting questions, and establishing a good atmosphere.

The moderator maintained the protocol for discussion, ensuring that everyone had an opportunity to speak so that no one person dominated the conversation. The teacher whose lesson was discussed did not participate in the main discussion but could make a closing statement, pointing out what he or she found striking or useful, and what he or she did or did not agree with. For example, one teacher said, "Your comments have helped me realize how little attention I pay to what is going on in my classroom. I would like to make my introductions more interesting, but I am often more focused on establishing discipline and taking attendance than on making the subject more interesting." This process of sharing gave us a chance to look at our work objectively and to construct new approaches to old problems.

Observing Two Students' Reactions

We also agreed to visit one another's classrooms to observe two different students selected by the teacher; each teacher chose one student that he or she believed was "good" and another perceived as "poor." We decided that such visits could take place only if two visiting teachers could observe together so that they could compare their opinions, and if the observed teacher agreed to the visit and its timing. To understand students' different responses, we discreetly observed these two students' reactions to teacher's questions, their levels of interest and engagement in the lesson, and the teacher's conduct. During our Critical Friends meetings, we discussed our observations. Some of the observations surprised the teachers. For example, visitors in several classrooms noticed that the student labeled as "poor" was often as actively involved in the lesson as the "good" student until he or she lost sight of the purpose of a particular activity. This observation helped the teachers realize how important it was to explain the goals of every activity. We found that the observers and teachers usually agreed on how well each teacher differentiated instruction and checked to make sure that every student was learning.

Sharing Difficulties

We also devoted a series of Critical Friends' meetings to analyzing difficult instructional problems presented by the participants. Each of us briefly defined the most serious problem he or she confronted in teaching, and the rest of the participants asked questions to understand each case. These questions asked by other participants helped the person with the problem to reconsider it from different perspectives.

One teacher, for example, described her difficulty with a student who behaved badly in class and did not focus on the lesson. After class one day, the student described to the teacher her personal problems and difficult home life. The teacher was torn between concern for the student and wariness that the student might be manipulating her emotions. The discussion explored the teacher's role in helping the student while maintaining standards for classroom conduct, and considered ways to work with the student's other teachers to resolve the situation.

Surveys of Students

Each of us conducted surveys of our students, asking them to express their disagreement or agreement on a scale of 1 (disagreement) to 6 (agreement) with such statements as "We learn useful information," "The class is organized in an interesting way," "Students have opportunities to voice their opinions," "The class has a friendly atmosphere," "The teacher grades according to known criteria," "The teacher is prepared for class," and "The teacher is interested in teaching this class." For most of us, this evaluation was the first we had ever conducted with students and the first collective, public discussion about how students perceive us. We proceeded carefully in our discussion, aware that such openness was revolutionary, and some of us chose to discuss our feelings about the results rather than the specific tallies. We agreed that the results did help us become more aware of how students felt about our classes and teaching methods.

The Results

Our readings and discussions helped us connect theory and practice and developed each member's sense of individual responsibility. Most important, we strengthened and deepened our trust in one another and received the support that we needed to develop our professional skills. For the first time since college, we talked about our work in an organized and methodical way. And by sharing our difficulties, we learned that we were not alone and that other teachers' perspectives can help us cope.

Even the best reforms may not work if teachers do not engage in constant, professional dialogue and build a learning culture of teachers who think about their practice. The traditional model of professional improvement—experts transferring knowledge—is not the most effective model. Cooperation among reflective practitioners examining one another's work is much more important. Many teachers feel embarrassed at first when they admit that they need help, but when they continue to meet in an atmosphere of openness and cooperation, they can improve.

Is our story one of great success and significant change in our school? Unfortunately not. Our school did not change just because a group of teachers wanted to do something more. Most of our school's changes occur on the surface—they are only cosmetic actions to cover stagnation. Now at the end of our second year, we struggle to maintain our level of energy and to enlarge the group. We agree that the process is important and we do not want to stop, but our efforts seem to be losing steam. We have not received any encouragement from the administrators or other teachers, who have closely observed us but have not reacted. The system allows us to operate with autonomy but does not encourage our efforts.

Has it been worth the effort? Probably yes, although we do not have any quantifiable proof. We do know, however, that it is beneficial to discuss important questions about our practice: Why do I teach in such a way? In what way will this exercise improve the competencies of my students? What kinds of research and theories are behind my style of teaching? In what way do I know what my students have learned? (Routman, 2002). Critical Friends has helped us in intangible ways. Only teachers, who know their professional goals and work, can take responsibility for this most difficult task: the success of every student.

References

Bambino, D. (2002). Critical friends. *Educational Leadership, 59*(6), 25–27.

Costa, A. L. (2001). Foreword. In J. York-Barr, W. A. Sommers, G. S. Ghere, & J. Montie (Eds.), *Reflective practice to improve schools: An action guide for educators* (pp. 13–16). Thousand Oaks, CA: Corwin.

Routman, R. (2002). Teacher talk. *Educational Leadership, 59*(6), 32–35.

20

Restoring the Joy of Teaching

Frank W. Powers

Frank W. Powers is an assistant professor at the University of Idaho–Coeur d'Alene, Division of Teaching, Learning, and Leadership, W. 1000 Hubbard Ave., Ste. 242, Coeur d'Alene, ID 83814. He can be reached by phone at (208) 667-2588 and by e-mail at fpowers@uidaho.edu.

I am a second-career teacher. Like most teachers, I entered the profession with a sense of altruism and the desire to make a difference in children's lives. But my new career almost came to an end before it had a chance to materialize. Five weeks into my first teaching assignment at a middle school, I wanted to quit. The atmosphere was cold and uncaring, with few smiles, little laughter, and virtually no opportunity to become part of the team. If not for the intervention of two experienced teachers, Stan and Steve, I would have become a statistic—one of the large percentage of teachers who leave the profession within their first five years.

In my previous career as a regional manager for a large restaurant chain, the culture of the workplace had been warm, friendly, and caring. Laughter and fun were embedded into the organizational climate. We worked as a team and produced results as a team. We celebrated accomplishments, promotions, and successes. We consoled one another in disappointments and setbacks. The "we" took precedence over any "I." We celebrated Mondays as the start of another opportunity to reach our goals, and we looked forward to each new challenge.

The contrast between these two environments does not mean that life in the business sector is better than life in the public education field. But as educators, we can and should learn some lessons from the best corporate environments about creating the kind of workplace that motivates employees and inspires them to perform at the highest levels.

Schools are the world's best source of potential success stories. No business success could ever equal the accomplishment of seeing one of your students experience an "Aha" moment in the classroom. As an educator, I had many opportunities to help students make good choices in their lives. What could be more important than having a positive influence on the life of a child? The chance to make a difference in a caring atmosphere is one of the most powerful rewards of teaching. Students, too, crave a nurturing school environment. But how can we create a culture in which teachers, students, and others feel free to express and accept caring?

A Lesson from the Ritz-Carlton

A few years ago I stayed at a Ritz-Carlton Hotel during a conference. As one would imagine, the aesthetics were wonderful. My enduring memory, however, is of the way in which the entire staff treated every guest. From the restaurant busboys to the managers, all were sensitive to each guest's needs and desires. Everyone seemed to know my name. The employees not only smiled at the guests and treated them pleasantly, but they were also polite, friendly, and courteous to one another. Laughter was the hotel's background music.

Something was happening behind the scenes that the guests could not see but that they could feel in the atmosphere. Somehow, the hotel had created a pervasive climate of warmth, comfort, caring, and fun.

After several days, my curiosity peaked and I asked one of the front-desk employees about the unusual attitudes of all the employees. "How do you do it?" I asked. "Do what, sir?" he responded. "How do you manage to get all the employees to treat your guests so well?" The reply was simple but profound: "You think we treat our guests well? You should see how we treat one another." I had one last question: "How do you get the employees to treat one another well?" The response: "We have fun!"

A School's Transformation

As I moved along in my career as a teacher, I found that schools could also foster a caring and fun environment. In fact, the school where I began my career eventually developed such a climate under the direction of a new principal. We realized that we needed to be kind to one another through such common courtesies as speaking, smiling, or even waving as we passed in the hall. Kindness also meant acknowledging the diversity of the staff and embracing our differences. We then examined our purpose for existence as a school and affirmed that we were there for the students, not for ourselves. This common purpose was a major unifying factor.

We learned about one another's talents and abilities. We found a wealth of talent and information at our immediate disposal. We eliminated the barriers to asking for help and became an interdependent school—a true team. The invisible boundaries began to dissolve.

Following the lead of the new principal, we decided to have fun and encourage laughter. We focused on the major issues, and the small stuff tended to disappear, or at least become less stressful. The words of a poster in one classroom became our motto: "Attitude is the mind's paintbrush; it colors any situation." From this point we decided to make a conscious choice to make the best of every day. The kindness, humor, recognition of talents, and respect for one another soon created a joyful environment.

A Place to Start

Schools that want to generate an atmosphere of joy must first examine the fun and caring factors within the school. To assess these factors, ask:

- Is laughter a common element in the school? Do you often hear laughter in the teachers lounge? Do teachers encourage students to laugh? One belly laugh a day is a good prescription for improved health and morale.
- Do the teachers acknowledge one another in the hall? Do they smile at one another?
- Do the teachers want to be here? Or do they start talking in October about how many days are left until summer vacation? Students can tell whether their teachers enjoy being with them and get satisfaction from teaching them.
- Is the school staff unified, or do teachers gather in cliques that exclude some teachers and admit others? Staff unity and collaboration are key requirements in establishing a caring environment.
- Do administrators and teachers treat substitute teachers well and welcome them like guests in a home, or are they left to fend for themselves?

Substitutes are professional guests. They form opinions about a school and talk to many other people. Word of mouth is a powerful source of information.

- Does the school have routines to help new teachers adapt? Does it welcome new individuals into the group and assign them mentors to help them fit in?

- Does the school have traditions to celebrate successes? Human beings need recognition and thrive in environments that celebrate both small and large successes.

- Does the school treat mistakes as learning experiences? Everyone makes mistakes. If teachers believe that "When I am right, no one remembers, and when I am wrong, no one forgets," then they will not dare to take risks.

- Does the school value innovation more than the status quo? Rigid rules and curriculums discourage teachers from trying research-based strategies to improve student learning. To create an innovative environment, we must give teachers the freedom to try new ideas. Innovation generally leads to an atmosphere of excitement and productivity.

If the answer to any of these questions is no, you may want to consider implementing the Ritz-Carlton model to increase the atmosphere of joy in your school.

The Importance of Leadership

Culture change in any organization usually begins with the leader. The tone and climate of the school reflects the education leader's values and actions. If the leader supports, demonstrates, and models caring and fun, the school will usually follow. Leadership by example is one of the most powerful means of rejuvenating an environment.

Each of us encounters hundreds of opportunities every day to model caring and fun. To create a school that supports these behaviors, start with yourself. Ask this simple question: How do my peers or subordinates perceive the way that I treat them? A few informal conversations can give you valuable information about the overall feelings of your school staff.

The change process will not happen overnight. It takes time to change a school's climate. Be patient and enlist the help of others by modeling the desired result. Set goals and formulate a plan to become a caring and fun school.

21

Sharing Knowledge, Sharing Leadership

Faith Spitz

Faith Spitz was superintendent of the Readington Township School District from 1996 to 2002 and is currently president of Technical Consulting Worldwide, 9 Sunnyfield Dr., Annandale, NJ 08801. She can be reached by phone at (908) 735-8274 and by e-mail at fspitz@att.net.

In an education market that suffers from a shortage of qualified teachers, Readington Township School District in New Jersey has been able to attract and retain superior staff through a commitment to ongoing professional development. Readington Township is a growing suburban, middle-class community. The district's 200 teachers provide instruction at four school sites serving about 2,300 students in grades PreK–8. Students in grades 9–12 attend a regional high school nearby.

Both new teachers and veterans come to Readington's schools because of the quantity and quality of the professional development experiences that our district provides. The district has built a community of learners committed to teacher recruitment, teacher retention, and teacher leadership. Readington has developed the kind of learning and leadership that Fullan envisions: "When there is widespread learning in context, leadership for the future is a natural by-product. Strong organizations have leaders at all levels" (2001, p. 133).

Guiding Principles for Change

Readington's current culture of teacher leadership began to evolve when we made a major change in our supervision model in 1996. Since then, we have developed a commitment as an organization to continual learning and improvement. The staff engages in frequent, focused conversations about teacher learning. Opportunities for self-reflection, collective inquiry, and sharing personal practice have increased. We have developed a common professional language, communal success stories, and extensive opportunities for quality professional development.

Our goal was to change the district culture into one in which staff and student learning would thrive. The cultural change process did not come quickly or easily, however. As guidelines for our change, we adopted the organizing principles of reform outlined by Elmore and Burney (1999). We decided to

- Focus on instruction.
- Recognize that instructional improvement is a long, multistage process involving awareness, planning, implementation, and reflection.
- Make shared expertise the driver of instructional change.
- Focus on systemwide improvement.
- Expect good ideas to come from talented people working together.
- Set clear expectations, and then decentralize.
- Make collegiality, caring, and respect paramount.

In our district, everyone is responsible for professional development. The board of education, the administrators, and the teaching staff are all deeply committed to their own learning in order to improve student learning. Teachers know that what they do counts.

Treating Teachers as Professionals

In 1996, after our review of the research found that our clinical model of supervision did little to improve instruction and student learning, we decided to examine alternative methods of supervision. The research suggested that teacher self-reflection based on quality teaching standards would lead to teacher improvement (Airasian & Gullickson, 1997; Barth, 1990; Danielson, 1996; Little, 1982; Talbert & McLaughlin, 1994). We decided to revise our supervision practices and allow teachers to take on the major responsibility of improving student learning (Spitz, 2001).

The role of our principals has changed dramatically. Although their job remains helping teachers to help students, they no longer conduct classroom observations of tenured teachers unless one of these teachers requests an observation to improve a targeted area, or has been identified as a teacher in need of assistance. Instead of being clinically supervised by the principal, each tenured staff member chooses an area for improvement and, with the principal, decides how he or she will provide evidence of growth in this area.

The teacher may choose to engage in action research, develop a portfolio, engage in peer coaching, design and implement a curriculum project, take part in a collegial partnership, or keep an interactive journal with an administrator or a peer. These options all involve teacher self-reflection as a major component. Our standards clearly define expectations about teaching (Danielson, 1996); our teachers have developed the standards and the board of education has approved them.

The new supervision model helped to build a heightened sense of trust between the board of education, administration, and staff. Supervision was no longer seen as a "gotcha" activity, but instead as a way to improve instruction and student learning. The new model treats teachers like professionals, and teachers have responded by becoming more reflective about the ways in which they can learn from one another. Giving and receiving help comes naturally within the context of daily instruction. For example, an elementary health and physical education teacher wrote:

> I really had no idea of what I was in store for when I began this year. I was surprised by the differences among the students as to what concepts they could grasp and what concepts needed a bit more explaining. There were times where I was discussing a topic and the students were giving me very quizzical looks. Being new to the field, I thought I was explaining the material on their level. After they still were not able to grasp it, I started to get a little flustered, not with the students but with myself because I thought I was using terms and situations that they could relate to. Fortunately, the classroom teacher would often remain in the class to finish up work. Knowing her students better than I did, she would offer to explain the concept I was beating myself up over. I would listen to how the teacher would describe it and remember it for later use. I found that if I used that teacher's way of describing the same concept in another class, students would grasp the concept much more quickly and save me the anxiety of second-guessing my teaching methods.

Developing a Community of Learners

The new supervision process challenged teachers to take more responsibility than ever before for their own professional growth. In return, the district put into place many structures to help the staff become a learning community.

Time for Growth

Each year, the board of education approves eight early dismissal days to provide staff development. These days are not one-shot events; they focus on district initiatives, which are established on a five-year cycle. In addition to the eight half-days, teachers have three full staff development days, also focused on the district's learning initiatives: two at the start of the school year, and one in February. Through this targeted, carefully planned staff development, staff members throughout the district's four schools share knowledge and create new understanding.

The staff development topics for the district's initiatives continue from year to year. A major focus has been differentiation of instruction—tailoring instruction to meet the individual needs of students. Teachers explore this topic through shared book discussions, teacher presentations, and keynote speakers followed by small-group discussions, which take place frequently at grade-level meetings, common planning time meetings, faculty meetings, half-day early dismissal days, and full-day staff development opportunities. A continuing education course on differentiated instruction has been offered after school for several years. To build teachers' levels of competence in working with all students, the district's differentiated instruction strategies encompass working with special education students. Other major staff development topics since 1996 have included the use of technology to enhance student learning, developmentally appropriate practices for K–2 students, thematic approaches to literature, inquiry science (in conjunction with a Merck partnership), and use of brain-based research to increase student performance.

Articulation between and across grades also takes place through common planning periods, which occur daily at the middle school and weekly at the elementary schools. The common planning time allows teachers to engage in meaningful conversations about instruction.

Continuing Education

The district provides courses each year that teachers can take for continuing education units. This year's course selections included the following:

- Thematic Approaches to Literature Instruction
- Educational Innovations
- The Teacher as the Professional
- Building Leadership Within
- Strategies for Reaching Students with Special Needs
- Teaching for Understanding: Backward Design Theory for the Middle School Classroom
- Putting It into Practice
- A Differentiation Workshop
- Developmentally Appropriate Practice for the K–2 Classroom
- Practical Implementation of Technology

Of our 200 teachers, 168 have participated in continuing education unit courses. Each teacher receives one credit on the salary guide or $250 for each course taken. Staff members may take up to three courses in any school year for credit or stipend. Several staff members have taken more than three courses because of their strong interest in the topics.

The district has further demonstrated its commitment to professional development by creating the position of teacher coach. We transferred one of our outstanding teachers out of the classroom and designated her as a staff development specialist. This person

- Coordinates the district's staff development programs in conjunction with principals, the assistant superintendent for curriculum and instruction, and the district's professional development committee.
- Helps teachers develop and teach continuing education courses.
- Visits and observes all new teachers, acting as a mentor and coach.
- Assists principals in working with tenured staff members who require assistance in order to meet the Readington Teacher Standards, offering suggestions and serving as a coach toward improving instructional design and implementation.

- Makes presentations and facilitates faculty meetings and half-day curriculum workshops, working closely with the building principals and assistant superintendent of curriculum and instruction.

Induction of New Teachers

The district holds a weeklong orientation session for all new staff members before they begin work in Readington. New teachers partner with trained mentors, and principals in each school hold monthly voluntary new-teacher seminars. All new teachers also take two continuing education unit courses: First Steps in the fall semester and Second Steps in the spring semester.

The First Steps class encompasses such topics as student discipline, establishing routines, holding parent conferences, "Back to School Night" planning, characteristics of an effective teacher and classroom, and a review of the core curriculum areas. New teachers become familiar with the teaching standards required for receiving tenure in the district. The class also provides a collegial and positive atmosphere in which to discuss problems that new teachers encounter.

In the Second Steps course, teachers deepen their knowledge of district initiatives. Teachers explore lesson planning using essential questions and a backward design model built around the question, "What do you want students to know and be able to do?" Participants work on the personal portfolios and reflections that all non-tenured staff are required to complete.

Shared Book Discussion

Each year, the entire professional staff and all board of education members read a professional "book of the year" selected by the district to enhance teacher performance and to improve student learning. Study and discussion of this book take place throughout the year at faculty meetings and common planning time meetings. Since the initiative began, we have studied the following books:

- 1997—*Enhancing Professional Practice* (1996), by Charlotte Danielson
- 1998—*How to Differentiate Instruction in Mixed-Ability Classrooms* (1995), by Carol Ann Tomlinson
- 1999—*The Differentiated Classroom* (1999), by Carol Ann Tomlinson

- 2000—*Teaching with the Brain in Mind (1998)*, by Eric Jensen
- 2001—*Understanding by Design (2000)*, by Grant Wiggins and Jay McTighe
- 2002—*A Mind at a Time (2002)*, by Mel Levine

Learning by Doing

> When we value craft knowledge, we develop a school culture hospitable to learning. A central part of the work of the school-based reformer is to find ways to honor, reveal, exchange, and celebrate the craft knowledge that resides in every schoolhouse. (Barth, 2001, p. 62)

The Readington staff has come to understand the value of learning by doing. Not only do the teachers' lessons reflect an understanding that students learn by doing, but the teachers themselves engage in action research and learn by doing.

Our teachers continually reflect on practice and then take action to find a better way. *Plan—do—check—act* has become a way of life. Teachers do not take action merely on the basis of what their principal, superintendent, or board of education tells them to do, but according to their own beliefs about what works, based on evidence.

For example, a tenured middle school math teacher conducted action research to determine whether a standards-based math program would improve mathematical learning for 6th grade students. Her research focused on how standards-based programs emphasizing student understanding, student-centered strategies, sharing, and discussion differ from traditional mathematics programs and what impact a standards-based program would have on student learning. At the end of the year, she wrote in her reflection:

> Assessment takes on a different form in standards-based programs. Students are required to apply strategies and to explain their ideas in writing. How the student arrived at the answer is an important component of the assessment. Students have made connections between mathematical ideas, have solved problems in a variety of ways, and have gained a wealth of strategies to use in solving problems. Using a standards-based program, I found I knew much more about my students' individual and collective knowledge than I could when using a traditional program. Through the assessment pieces that I used,

the students clearly had a meaningful experience and gained a depth of knowledge much greater than they would have gained from a traditional approach.

Based on the pilot study of a standards-based mathematics program, I will recommend that the math curriculum committee adopt one of the standards-based programs for district use. These programs provide rich experiences in which students develop meaning. Students are highly motivated and are able to communicate high levels of mathematical understanding. Other standards-based mathematics programs should be reviewed to evaluate their effectiveness with our students.

External Resources

We have been fortunate as a district to enlist major corporations in our area as partners. A partnership with Merck Pharmaceuticals, which has continued for almost a decade, provides professional development in using an inquiry-based approach to learning science, math, and technology. Merck has provided ongoing, sustained professional development that allows our teaching staff to work with well-known experts and participate in co-facilitated, weeklong learning experiences that simulate classroom instruction for students. Teachers have opportunities to engage in rich dialogue and experimentation to enrich their students' classroom learning.

In 2002, we formed a new partnership with Chubb & Sons Insurance Company that provides staff development opportunities for our team leaders using approaches developed with corporate executives.

Leadership Matters

Our teachers frequently attend national and state conferences and workshops to learn new ideas and strategies that support our initiatives. When they return, they facilitate continuing education unit courses and share their knowledge.

Teachers also have opportunities to serve as leaders by serving as peer coaches or mentors. In peer coaching, two experienced teachers work together to solve an instructional problem. Teachers observe each other and come up with alternative methods of improving instruction. Mentoring pairs a beginning teacher with an experienced teacher who exhibits distinguished performance. The weekly schedule allows time for a collaborative relationship to develop. Mentor teachers receive a small stipend for the extra time required.

The leadership roles played by teachers help to deepen their understanding of their own practice and make them more reflective as professionals. At the end of one year, a 1st grade teacher wrote:

> In rereading my previous self-reflections, I saw again the power that my prior experiences have had in influencing the place in which I am today. . . . Peer coaching brought out my self-confidence about teaching. The coaching experience enabled me to not only believe in what I was doing but also to stand up for what I believe. . . . Applying the skills I had developed as a peer coach to a mentoring relationship is a natural extension. Engaging in such in-depth professional development has forced me to become self-reflective about everything I do, not only with the students but with my colleagues as well.

As the superintendent of Readington, I always told the staff, "The *we* is smarter than the *me*." No one person can make institutional change happen. When we share our knowledge, more leaders emerge and the institution moves toward higher quality.

Teachers Make a Difference

The opportunity to express creativity and to share professional knowledge leads to sustained lifelong learning for all. In Readington Township School District, each teacher is a change agent responsible for continual improvement in the organization.

Our staff development program has changed the way our teachers think about themselves, their work, and their school. Our teachers and administrators take pride in sharing their insights into teaching and learning as they make presentations at board of education meetings, state and national conventions, and other conferences and workshops. We have created a district culture that empowers teachers to become learners, and to recognize that they make a difference in their classrooms, in our district, and in the field of education.

References

Airasian, P. W., & Gullickson, A. R. (1997). *Teacher self-evaluation tool kit.* Thousand Oaks, CA: Corwin.

Barth, R. (1990). *Improving schools from within.* San Francisco: Jossey-Bass.

Barth, R. (2001). *Learning by heart.* San Francisco: Jossey-Bass.

Danielson, C. (1996). *Enhancing professional practice: A framework for teaching.* Alexandria, VA: Association for Supervision and Curriculum Development.

Elmore, R. F., & Burney, D. (1999). Investing in teacher learning: Staff development and instructional improvement. In L. Darling-Hammond & G. Sykes (Eds.), *Teaching as the learning profession: Handbook of policy and practice* (pp. 236–291). San Francisco: Jossey-Bass.

Fullan, M. (2001). *Leading in a culture of change.* San Francisco: Jossey-Bass.

Little, J. W. (1982). Norms of collegiality and experimentation: Workplace conditions of school success. *American Educational Research Journal, 19*(3), 325–40.

Spitz, F. (2001). Through the looking glass: Teacher evaluation through self-reflection. *New Jersey Journal of Supervision and Curriculum Development, 45,* 13–21.

Talbert, J., & McLaughlin, M. (1994). Teacher professionalism in local school contexts. *American Journal of Education, 102*(2), 123–153.

22

Are You a Morale Booster ... or Buster?

Martha Jo Price

Martha Jo Price is a French and English teacher in the Smyth County Schools, Virginia. She can be reached by phone at (276) 782-3686 and by e-mail at mjprice53@hotmail.com.

School shootings, vandalism, drug and alcohol abuse, understaffing, over-crowding—many problems plague our public schools today. Yet most schools in the United States remain vibrant, happy places where meaningful learning takes place. The most productive schools depend on thoughtful, sensitive administrators who support their teachers and allow enthusiasm for learning to spread throughout the building. Every school has some problems, but the principal who has a positive demeanor, a good sense of humor, and a genuine love of students and staff does much to eliminate these problems.

In my long career in the classroom, I have worked with eight principals and 12 assistant principals. Each one employed different techniques in dealing with his or her constituencies. Some were successful; some failed miserably. I began to mentally categorize these principals into two groups: morale boosters and morale busters. The morale-boosting administrators employed most of the following techniques.

Empower Your Teachers and Student Leaders

As human beings, we always work harder when we feel a sense of ownership. We have all known the teacher who stays in his or her classroom, fearful of breaking a rule or getting in trouble. This teacher feels powerless to effect school change, does nothing to ripple the waters, and consequently becomes more impotent as time passes.

We have also known the proverbial ball of fire who seems to have a hand in everything, is busy all the time, and gives his or her best for students and fellow staff members. Cathy is such a person. As art teacher at the local high school, she was busy preparing for homecoming activities this week. She tie-dyed more than 150 T-shirts for students, made a gigantic fabric flag to hang from the top of the stadium, and painted intricate designs on the football field—in addition to teaching five art classes filled to overflowing, transporting her two children to their own extracurricular activities, and helping her husband manage a minor-league baseball team in town.

What keeps teachers like Cathy so involved? What makes the difference in their approach to their job? The attitude of their principal makes a big contribution. Most teachers will go to the ends of the earth for an administrator who allows them to share in decision making. My favorite administrator was a proponent of site-based management. He allowed his teachers to help with departmental scheduling, student scheduling, and duty assignments. He realized that he would have to listen to far less grumbling about decisions made *by* teachers than about decisions made *for* teachers.

One can easily distinguish the teachers who feel empowered. They take pride in the accomplishments of their students. They consider themselves keepers of the building, often bending down to pick up trash or donning an apron to help serve in the cafeteria when the lunch line backs up. They are consistently animated and involved.

Model a Caring Attitude

To lead effectively, you must supplement the innate power of your position as principal with personal power: job-specific knowledge, love of people, and common sense. Teachers often perceive the administrator who resorts to the banal "because I'm the boss" attitude as a failure.

Be on time and always be dependable. Make sure that teachers can contact you throughout the day, even if just by walkie-talkie. Let teachers know that they can also call you at home. Sometimes in the course of a busy school day, a teacher just cannot get in to see you.

Be a good listener. No matter how busy you are, stand still while someone is talking to you; better yet, sit down to signal the importance of the conversation. Put the paperwork aside, and as one of my favorite administrators always did, turn off the telephone. Don't glance over the shoulder of the person speaking to you as if you are anticipating the next person demanding more of your time. Give your full attention to the person you're talking to.

Get to Know Your Staff

People feel valued when an administrator takes the time to learn their hobbies, their achievements, and their children's and spouse's names. If you're new to the staff, have veteran faculty members keep you informed about faculty news. Inquire about the husband's surgery; spread the word about the child's scholarship or touchdown; make an announcement about the article published by the English teacher. Nothing boosts morale more than the personal touch.

One excellent way to open the lines of communication and let staff members know that you value their opinions is to schedule periodic "lunch with the principal" sessions. Invite teachers to your office during their lunch periods on a rotating basis and treat them to a special dessert and private talk time.

Put a thank you note in the mailbox of the teacher who planned the student assembly; take late duty for the teacher with a doctor's appointment; give a book bag filled with helpful tools and resources to each new teacher; hold a drawing each month for dinners at a local restaurant. These simple actions show your faculty members that you appreciate everything they do. In return, they will appreciate you.

Catch People Doing Something Good

Anyone in administration should remember the old adage "Praise in front of others; criticize in private." Nothing is more humiliating than having one's faults pointed out in a faculty meeting or in an office filled with other teachers and students; yet we have all seen insensitive administrators do it, apparently in an attempt to gain submission through intimidation.

Close your office door whenever you need to discuss a problem with a teacher. For serious issues, have another administrator present. On the other hand, when someone has done something exceptional, write a congratulatory note and post it prominently on the outside of his or her mailbox, inviting everyone on the staff to add his or her congratulations to yours. Make sure to catch each staff member doing something good at least once in the school year.

Create a User-Friendly School

Do your teachers have private, conveniently located restrooms? Do they have access to a private phone that they can use to make appointments, check on a sick child, or transfer bank funds? Do teachers have a quiet place where they can congregate just to put their feet up, have a cup of coffee, and take a breather for a few minutes?

The teachers lounge has developed negative connotations through the years, and I must admit that I taught at one school where the lounge was labeled the "viper pit." The moment the door was closed, a small group of negative staff members would begin dismantling a colleague's reputation, dissecting a student's home life, and verbally attacking everything good and fruitful in the school. In my present school, however, teachers gather in a well-stocked workroom next to the guidance office where they can have a soda, talk to one another, consult guidance records, or make copies. Although faculty members seldom stay longer than 15 minutes, this time often provides just the break they need to get through the day.

Keep soap, tissues, lotions, and magazines in faculty restrooms. Have a well-stocked coffee closet in the workroom. Keep several large umbrellas in the office for teachers serving bus duty, and always have a spare set of jumper cables available for dead batteries on snowy afternoons.

Maintain an up-to-date professional library in the workroom or office. Ask your school librarian to copy pertinent articles for each teacher's box. Display travel brochures and announcements of teacher-directed tours that come in the school mail. Start a book exchange shelf where teachers can share their favorite fiction with one another.

Finally, offer ample opportunity for out-of-school socializing, which gives the staff time together to unwind away from the daily routine. Many faculties have monthly potluck dinners for staff members and their families. Obviously, not everyone can attend every gathering, but most people will try to come from time to time.

Keep in Touch

Each of the key characteristics of morale-boosting principals depends on staying in touch with the entire school staff. To be a morale booster, learn to assess the atmosphere in the school and the mental well-being of your teachers. Listen to what the staff says and thoughtfully consider suggestions placed in your mailbox.

Learning that takes place in a happy atmosphere is more likely to stay with students for the rest of their lives. Who ever said that teaching and learning shouldn't be fun? Make it obvious that you enjoy your job, and your teachers will follow suit.

23

Our Rodney Dangerfield Profession

Paul Thomas

Paul Thomas is an assistant professor of education at Forman University in Greenville, South Carolina. He can be reached by phone at (864) 294-3386 and by e-mail at paul.thomas@furman.edu.

This is the story of a wonderful young teacher who was mistreated. Unfortunately, young teachers have little or no voice in the teaching profession, even less than veteran teachers have. If the education field hopes to recruit and retain outstanding professional educators, much has to change. The rocky beginning that this teacher endured illustrates the changes that we need to make.

Painful Awakenings

Let's call the teacher Edna, after the main character in Kate Chopin's *The Awakening* (1899)—although her eventual fate is better than that of the tragic character in the novel. An ambitious student in public school and college, Edna had always been a voracious consumer of books. After racing through college, she found herself teaching elementary school. She worked selflessly and relentlessly during that first year of teaching.

The summer after her first year, she enrolled in a National Writing Project Summer Institute that I cotaught. Edna dove into the course with infectious enthusiasm. Her showcase presentation was a whirlwind event highlighting everything she had done in her incredibly active classroom the year before. It was an amazing display—but, unfortunately, a display of what *not* to do. Edna exhibited an enthusiastic but uninformed approach to teaching children to read and write.

My co-instructor and I said as gently as possible, "That was beautifully done, Edna, but . . ." Then we began a lengthy discussion of the disparity between her teacher-driven, skills-intensive practices and the best practices supported by research.

Edna could easily have folded at that moment, or simply rejected our guidance, but she didn't. That summer became a professional and personal awakening for her. Within weeks, she transformed herself into a student of best practices and an advocate for the effective teaching of reading and writing. From that summer on, she practiced what she preached. Edna's classroom evolved into a student-centered place where student choice and student voice were encouraged and valued. When Edna allowed her students to choose what they read and to choose their own topics and forms in writing, they became impressive readers and writers.

But more pain lay ahead for Edna. Far from receiving collegial support for her renewed efforts, this revitalized second-year teacher faced direct and consistent antagonism. Both her administrators and her peers rejected her new scholarship.

When Edna raced to her peers with her newfound ideas and interests, their immediate responses were buckets of cold water thrown on her fire: "Yeah, yeah, Edna, that sounds great, but none of it works in the real classroom. Don't waste your time. It's just too much work."

In her school, Edna faced a culture of conformity where teachers worked within the structure created by the principal. Instead of joining a collegial and professional dynamic, Edna became the "oddball," as she called herself—the teacher to whom the principal referred in condescending and belittling ways. Any teacher who dared to experiment or question the school's established practices was quickly and publicly ostracized. In short, Edna's principal and her peers failed her—creating a situation ripe for losing a wonderful young teacher.

Roadblocks to Change

The summer institute had been like a religious renewal for Edna. She had found a supportive group of teachers and colleagues who knew about best practices and wanted other teachers to grow as people and professionals. She felt a moral imperative to give each student the best education she could, knowing that literacy was their greatest hope for healthy and happy lives.

Why did veteran teachers in Edna's school fail to support her professional growth and reject the insights that she offered? Here are a few of the conditions that typically make meaningful educational change nearly impossible and that make retaining good teachers so difficult.

Distrust of research and statistics. During my career, I have heard many teachers sweep aside research on best practices by saying, "You can make research say anything you want." If we are to improve education and empower teachers to improve their effectiveness, we must address this weakness in teacher preparation and renewal. Educators must have a better understanding of the value of research, including the difference between a single study and a body of research and the value of the research model as a guide for classroom practice.

Far too many teachers have been assaulted by research presented as dogma, rather than as a body of evolving understandings that require teachers to experiment. Like most teachers, Edna desired a supportive environment in which she could implement best practices in reading and writing—an environment where teaching and learning were organic, evolving endeavors. Instead she found intellectual stasis, bureaucratic conformity, and a pervasive nonscholarly atmosphere.

A "don't bother" stance that rejects new methods simply because they take more time and effort. Schools too often determine what approaches to implement on the basis of which ones are the most manageable. Scripted lesson plans, lockstep classroom practices, and quickly scored assessments are easy to do and easy to standardize—but do they contribute to students' understanding? When schools don't give teachers the opportunity or the encouragement to act as reflective practitioners, many teachers will somewhat mindlessly tick along in their jobs and contribute to an atmosphere that stifles other teachers who are more energetic, and more reflective.

Edna's principal frequently reprimanded her for not maintaining a standardized course of instruction. The school required all teachers at the same grade level to do the same things at the same times. None of Edna's peers voiced any opposition to this practice. Her school did not offer any professional avenue for her to present her research-based objections or for teachers to discuss the merits of any practice. Instead, Edna was forced to either conform or be subversive.

Reluctance to relinquish power. A disturbing dynamic that makes education and educators so recalcitrant to change is the issue of power. A couple of years ago, I was fortunate enough to attend a Writing Project retreat where several women educators informally discussed power. Their conclusion: Because education has a history as a women's profession, the teacher's power status is often muted. Many teachers feel that they have only one avenue of power—behind the closed doors of their classrooms. These teachers may view the ideas and experiments proposed by new teachers as criticisms of their own methods and attacks on their own power.

Too often, department and grade-level politics, a pointless fight for turf and power, inhibit classroom change that would benefit student learning. To recruit and retain the best and brightest teachers, schools must become collegial communities that acknowledge young teachers as valued contributors to the profession.

An atmosphere that deters authentic teaching and learning. Regardless of state or district mandates, regardless of the abilities and motivation of a faculty, the greatest influence on the real workings of a school is the principal. Edna endured numerous obstacles put in place by a misguided principal.

Edna's school is beautiful. On many occasions, the principal has spoken of the public relations efforts that the school needs to implement to recruit the right kinds of families and students to move into the neighborhood. The principal believes that if the school has a strong public image, real estate agents will pass on the word to potential home buyers, and builders and contractors will create high-income housing in the attendance area. In an era of standards and accountability, this principal has decided that the key to success is filling the building with high-achieving children from the best homes. Then scores will soar!

Many other principals unfortunately settle for superficial excellence, assuming that quiet classrooms are good classrooms, and that desks in rows and students in line are signs of an effective teacher. The message may come overtly or covertly, but teachers know when the principal honors and supports the *appearance* of good schooling more than actual effective teaching and learning.

Manipulation of teacher appraisals. All of us wish for job security; all of us hope that our abilities and performance will earn that security. Unfortunately, both new and veteran teachers sometimes have their appraisals and their contracts held over their heads—especially if they begin to swim against the stream. Just as students often learn to become passive and quiet so that they will be viewed as good students, teachers learn to do as they are told—or at least appear to do as they are told. Such passivity runs counter to being a successful educator and to being a scholar and a professional.

Dictation of teacher behavior. Edna and her peers were often told what and how to teach. As mentioned before, the school dictated that all students in any grade be taught in standardized ways and on identical timetables. Had teachers created this program? Had the school explored research to support such a practice? No and no. Strict state and federal mandates have led increasing numbers of schools to stress direct teaching and testing of the content of high-stakes tests. Apparently, teaching directly to the test feels safe and productive.

More teachers—both young and experienced—are leaving the profession. Luckily, many of the best and brightest do remain in our field, but I fear that the trend toward losing more good teachers will grow. What can reverse this trend?

Edna's Happy Continuing

First, let's celebrate Edna's happy ending—or, more appropriately, her continuing, since her career is really just beginning. Edna's fate as a teacher has taken a decided turn for the better. Two events played key roles.

After spending a summer as a co-instructor of teachers in connection with an affiliate of the National Writing Project—an important affirmation of her professionalism—Edna faced a new challenge in her third year of teaching. Her principal proposed a plan to group students according to their reading abilities in hopes of raising state assessment scores in language arts. A similar strategy had been used the year before in math, and scores had risen.

Edna knew that the plan would violate best practices in teaching reading and writing. She voiced her concerns; then she went into action. Edna gathered all the research literature she could on addressing reading weaknesses in elementary children. She distributed the materials to both her principal and all her fellow teachers in hopes that they would recognize the negative effects of grouping for reading instruction.

When Edna contacted me for advice, I told her that she was wasting her time (wasn't that supportive of me?), but encouraged her to make the effort anyway. Edna called a few weeks later. Amazingly, her school had scrapped the plan to group students by reading ability. The principal had reluctantly deferred to the body of evidence.

Not long after this victory for Edna—and the students—she learned that her peers had selected her as the school's reading teacher of the year and then as district reading teacher of the year. Edna was elated. Both as a young woman and as a young professional, she felt validated and empowered. And fortunately for her students, she has renewed her commitment to education.

What Can Schools Do?

Johnson and Kardos (2002) recognize the pivotal role that mentor teachers, veteran colleagues, and principals play in the induction years of new teachers:

> What new teachers want in their induction is experienced colleagues who will take their daily dilemmas seriously, watch them teach and provide feedback, help them develop instructional strategies, model skilled teaching, and share insights about students' work and lives. What new teachers need is sustained, school-based professional development—guided by expert colleagues, responsive to their teaching, and continual throughout their early years in the classroom. Principals and teacher leaders have the largest roles to play in fostering such experiences. (p. 13)

New teachers need to be empowered by their principals and their peers. They need to remain active learners and scholars themselves. They need to be treated as professionals and to act as professionals.

A growing voice among both the populace and the politicians says that anyone can teach—that to improve schools, all we need is competition, high standards, scripted curriculum, and high-stakes tests. These remedies are all wrong. To improve education, schools need to recruit and retain teachers of the highest quality. And doing that will require changing the essential fabric of the education field:

- We must expect educators at all levels and in all positions to become scholars, and we must hold them to the highest standards of scholarship and professionalism. Doctors control the medical field, business leaders direct the business field, and lawyers direct the legal system. Educators must rise to a similar status within education.

- We must face head-on the political drive to value the surface over the substance in education. Quiet students and malleable teachers do not a good school make. As scholars, teachers must become political; we must assert our expertise in the governance of our field.

- Administrators and teachers must accept and demonstrate that teaching with best practices, teaching holistically and authentically, will yield higher test scores, even on narrow and standardized tests. We must not continue to allow the methods that we know are best to be shoved aside out of fear fueled by misguided and poorly implemented accountability measures.

At the end of Chopin's *The Awakening*, the fictional Edna drowns herself in despair—an apt and disturbing metaphor for the many educators who give up and leave education because they have been denied the self-determination, respect, and empowerment that all professionals deserve. Fortunately, some determined young teachers like Edna refuse to abandon their profession and their students, in spite of the barriers they face. They persist and find colleagues to share their vision. Let's hope that we can all stand together and learn to surf the waves that crash against us.

References

Chopin, K. (1899). *The Awaking.* Chicago: H. S. Stone & Company.

Johnson, S. M., & Kardos, S. M. (2002). Keeping new teachers in mind. *Educational Leadership, 59*(6), 13.

Part V

Reflecting on What Makes Good Teachers

What Keeps Teachers Going?

Sonia M. Nieto

Sonia M. Nieto is Professor of Language, Literacy, and Culture, Department of Teacher Education and Curriculum Studies, University of Massachusetts at Amherst, Amherst, MA 01003-9308. Her most recent book is What Keeps Teachers Going? *(Teachers College Press, 2003). She can be reached via e-mail at snieto@educ.umass.edu. This article originally appeared in the May 2003 issue of* Educational Leadership.

As a Puerto Rican child from a working-class family, I attended poor schools in Brooklyn, New York, where a small but significant number of teachers helped propel my sister and me—who were the first in our family to graduate from high school—to attend college and become teachers.

As a teacher educator and former classroom teacher, I have become increasingly concerned about the tenuous situation of the most vulnerable students in U.S. public schools—students who attend urban schools with crumbling infrastructures, few resources, and a highly mobile staff. For these students—primarily African American and Latino, but also poor students of all backgrounds—the teachers who believe in and push them, who refuse to accept anything less than the best from them, often make the single greatest difference between a life of hope and one of despair. In many cases, these are veteran teachers who have dedicated their professional careers—and, in many cases, their personal lives—to young people in urban schools.

Unfortunately, many of the most highly qualified and gifted teachers do not teach in the schools where their skills are most sorely needed. Poor students of color are at the bottom of the ladder for receiving services from the most-qualified teachers (Darling-Hammond, 1998).

Moreover, even though most teachers enter the profession for noble reasons and with great enthusiasm, many of those in urban schools know little about their students and find it hard to reach them. Thus, despite their good intentions, many teachers who work with students of racial and cultural backgrounds different from their own have limited experience in teaching them, and become frustrated and angry at the conditions in which they must work. Nearly half of all new teachers in urban public schools quit within five years (Haycock, 1998). The teacher dropout rate is certainly not new, but with the predicted looming teacher shortage, recruiting and retaining excellent teachers who are excited about and committed to teaching students in urban schools is more urgent than ever.

Why Do They Stay?

What keeps teachers going—in spite of everything? In 1999–2000, I collaborated with a small group of seven urban teachers in the Boston Public Schools to consider this important question.[1] Our inquiry group comprised highly respected high school teachers who had a reputation of success with students of diverse backgrounds. They teach math, English, health, and African American Studies in both monolingual English and bilingual settings. Their own backgrounds are quite diverse—African American, Cape Verdean, Haitian, Irish American, and Jewish, among others. Collectively, they have many years of experience; most have been teaching for more than 25 years. They have received numerous awards—five have been named Boston Teacher of the Year—and they are active in professional organizations, writing and reading groups, and other professional activities. They are also known to be movers and shakers, willing to speak up and take a stand.

Besides addressing this question during our meetings, we also read a number of books together and wrote narratives, letters, and e-mails to one another. The teachers spoke movingly about the joys, frustrations, and rewards of teaching. Our conversations were not easy, nor did they come close to solving the problems of urban schools. But the process helped articulate some reasons that these teachers have stayed in teaching, and transcripts of our meetings, writings, and field notes revealed several interrelated themes (Nieto, 2003).

---

[1] Ceronne Daly, then head of high school restructuring for the Boston Public Schools, helped organize the group. Members of the inquiry group who met throughout the year were Judith Baker, Claudia Bell, Sonie Felix, Karen Gelzinis, Stephen Gordon, Ambrizeth Lima, and Junia Yearwood.

This group of excellent urban teachers might seem to be the exception to the rule. As we have shared our thoughts with educators around the United States, however, we have found that teachers in many different situations—in schools small or large, elementary or secondary, urban or rural—have stayed in teaching for many of the same reasons.

Autobiography

Teachers' identities are deeply implicated in their teaching, and hence in their perseverance. Their identities are defined not only by ethnicity, race, gender, social class, and language background, although these all are significant. What became clear was that most of these teachers have been involved in movements for social justice. These included movements outside education (civil rights, anti-apartheid) as well as inside education (bilingual education, multicultural education, desegregation).

As a young child in Barbados, English teacher Junia Yearwood learned the value of education early on. She could not divorce her heritage and experiences from the reasons she came to school every day to teach:

> The value of education and the importance of being able to read and write became clear and urgent when I became fully aware of the history of my ancestors. The story of the enslavement of Africans and the horrors they were forced to endure repulsed and angered me, but the aspect of slavery that most intrigued me was the systematic denial of literacy to my ancestors. As a child of 10 or so, I reasoned that if reading and writing were not extremely important, then there would be no need to withhold those skills from the supposed "savage and inferior" African. I concluded that teaching was the most important profession on earth and that the teacher was the Moses of people of African descent. This revelation made my destiny clear. I had to be a teacher.

Love

It seems old-fashioned to speak of teaching as love, yet teachers in the inquiry group often used this word to describe how they feel about their students and the subject matter that they teach. Teacher Stephen Gordon observed that preceding everything else in teaching is "a fundamental belief in the lives and minds of students." Love, then, is not simply a sentimental conferring of emotion. Rather, it is a combination of trust, confidence, and faith in students and a deep admiration for their strengths.

These teachers demonstrate love through high expectations and rigorous demands on students, and by keeping up with their subject matter through professional activities. Claudia Bell, a bilingual teacher of Latino students, provides an example. For the first time in her career, she found that most of the students in her health class were failing. With the help of other colleagues in the inquiry group, she developed a questionnaire to try to figure out why. She discovered that the interview process brought the students and her closer together.

"I always thought I had a really close relationship with them," she explained. "But somehow, through this process, they opened up to me in ways that I didn't expect."

Within weeks, her students were doing their homework much more consistently, and their schoolwork in general improved. Claudia didn't see this as a miracle cure for low achievement. In fact, it initially bothered her that they were doing these things to please her rather than for themselves. But it also became clear to us that developing a closer relationship with the students had paid off. By the end of the year, many of the students were passing her course.

These teachers also believe in affirming their students' identities. Ambrizeth Lima, who came to the United States from the Cape Verde Islands when she was a child, points out that students should not have to "discard themselves" to be accepted. She encouraged her students, all of whom were from Cape Verde, to hold on to their language and to feel pride in their culture. More than most, she knows that students' identities do not disappear simply because schools refuse to acknowledge them. Teachers' caring promotes an essential sense of belonging for students whose backgrounds differ from the mainstream.

Hope and Possibility

Hope is the essence of teaching, and these teachers demonstrate hope in many ways. They have hope and faith in their students, in their own abilities as teachers, in trusted colleagues and new teachers, in the promise of public education, and in the profession of teaching.

One day, Judith Baker discussed the boys in her classes, mostly African American and Latino, who she knew were capable of doing well in school but were failing. "I'm very, very worried about the boys," she said. But rather than blame the situation on their laziness or lack of intelligence, she said with the greatest confidence, "I'm sure that these guys can do far better than they are, absolutely, positively." And she did everything to see that they would.

Another day, I met with a group of teachers with whom Junia had asked me to speak about what sustained them in teaching. They volunteered that what kept them engaged, in spite of the frustration and heartache they sometimes experienced, were student teachers who contributed new ideas; colleagues to whom they could turn for support; new teachers who came into the profession with lots of enthusiasm; and students who had graduated and come back to visit. Juan Figueroa, a relatively new teacher, gave an example.

"I was lucky enough to teach a class of seniors," he said. "This is the first year when they'll be graduating from college. Knowing that they're going to be graduating this year, and that two of them are going to be teachers, is incredible. They will be entering a profession that I love, and they'll be doing the same thing."

Anger and Desperation

One of the big surprises to emerge from my work with the inquiry group was the level of anger expressed by these excellent teachers. But I came to realize that anger is the other side of hope, and given the conditions in which they work, their hope is constantly tested.

The teachers were angry at the injustices their students have to endure, including racism and poverty. They were impatient with the arbitrariness of society; baffled at school policies made by people far removed from the daily realities of classroom life; and indignant at being treated as if they were children. But no matter how angry they were, they never expressed their frustration in mean-spirited comments about their students. Judith Baker explained, "I would exclude all 'social work' remedies. This is typical talk that teachers always do that leads nowhere." Judith was referring to the vain search for remedies to poverty and other social ills brought on by inequality. Nor did the teachers let their anger interfere with teaching. Junia Yearwood explained that her classroom was her haven. Once she entered the classroom, she said, "What I try to keep focused on is my kids, the students."

Sometimes, however, anger could spill over into desperation. Sonie Felix, the youngest member of the group, came in one day seriously considering leaving the profession. Although she enjoyed teaching and loved her students, she felt that she did not receive support or the opportunity to grow as an individual. She asked plaintively, "But what happens when that job is your life and calling? What do you do then?" The anger and resentment Sonie felt is not uncommon. Nevertheless, I am happy to report that Sonie is still teaching three years later—primarily because of the support of colleagues and her continuing participation in the intellectual life of teaching.

Intellectual Work

Engaging with trusted colleagues in what teacher Stephen Gordon called "adult conversations about unasked questions" is one way in which teachers do intellectual work. When we first started meeting as an inquiry group, I could see the impatience in Sonie's eyes. She wanted us to do something, not just talk. By our last meeting, Sonie had developed not only a desire, but also a need to talk. "I think that these conversations are important in terms of continuing with teaching," she said. "*That's* how and why people tend to leave, because these conversations don't happen."

In addition to participating in the inquiry group, these teachers took part in individual and collaborative curriculum development, wrote journals, conducted research in their classrooms, attended conferences, were active members in professional organizations, and mentored new colleagues. They also presented workshops for colleagues and visited other schools. In short, these teachers are constantly updating their craft and their knowledge.

Democratic Practice

Students in urban public schools face many problems, but discussions of these problems often place sole responsibility on the children and their families, as if the problems had sprung full-blown from them alone. Rather than the children lacking will or being of unsound moral character, it is the schools that often lack the will and the resources to teach these children. Any teacher who works in an urban school system can testify to this fact. A commitment to social justice—the ideals of democracy, fair play, and equality—figures prominently among the reasons why these teachers chose this profession.

I asked the teachers in the inquiry group to write a letter to an imaginary new teacher. What would a new teacher need to know? Stephen Gordon expressed the profound desire to engage in democratic practice:

> I am happy that I found a profession that combines my belief in social justice with my zeal for intellectual excellence. My career choice has meant much anxiety, anger, and disappointment. But it has also produced profound joy. I have spent my work life committed to a just cause: the education of Boston high school students. Welcome to our noble teaching profession and our enduring cause.

The Ability to Shape the Future

Teachers' words and actions are of greater consequence than those of almost any other profession. Karen Gelzinis, who had been Sonie Felix's algebra teacher 14 years before, reflected on the power of teaching:

> We change lives forever. Of course, we all know it. But how often do we really think about it? Does it get lost in the piles of paper that we correct? In the scores/grades that we write down? . . . I thought about the teachers I had had, who saw something in "the disadvantaged kids" from the city and gave us the hope that we could do whatever we wanted, and we could do it without giving up who we were. We didn't have to move to the suburbs to be successful.

> We [teachers] need different words to speak about what we do. Standards. Rubrics. Benchmarks. Ninth grader. Important words, yes. But these words do not tell the complete stories of our kids. So, despite everything in our way, why do some of us end up staying? Is it because our lives continue to be changed forever, for the better, by our students? What would my life be without Sonie, without Jeramie? . . . It is an addictive thing, teaching.

The Promise

The promise of public education is a seductive hope. Precisely because of the grim conditions in schools and society, a vigorous commitment to high-quality public education is more necessary than ever. In the past two decades, however, schools have undergone a period of constant reform and restructuring, and the talk surrounding public education has become mean-spirited and antagonistic, giving greater attention to vouchers, "choice," charter schools, and winner-take-all high-stakes tests as the only viable solutions to the crisis in public education. The result is a near wholesale abandonment of the public schools, especially those that serve poor children.

To keep good teachers, we must find ways to achieve the unfulfilled promise of public education. We must rethink teacher education so that it focuses on preparing teachers to work with enthusiasm, competence, and caring among the students in our urban schools. We must prepare teachers—not for missionary work, but for public service. We must rethink professional development—not as a way to fill teachers' heads with new and innovative ideas that may come and go, but rather as an approach that builds on teachers' professionalism and encourages their intellectual activity. Paradoxically, current reforms that focus only on accountability—including standardized testing, teacher testing, and other such policies—may be driving out some of the teachers who are effective with the students who most need committed and caring teachers.

If we are as concerned about education as we say we are, then we need to do more to change the conditions faced by teachers, especially those who work in underfinanced and largely abandoned urban schools. We need to support those teachers who love their students, who find creative ways to teach them, and who do so under difficult circumstances. We need to celebrate teachers who are as excited about their own learning as they are about the learning of their students. And we need to champion those teachers who value their students' families and find respectful ways to work with them. Above all, we need to expect all teachers to do these things. The children in our public schools deserve no less.

References

Darling-Hammond, L. (1998). Teachers and teaching: Testing policy hypotheses from a national commission report. *Educational Researcher, 27*(1), 5–15.

Haycock, K. (1998). No more settling for less. *Thinking K–16, 4*(1), 3–12.

Nieto, S. (2003). *What keeps teachers going?* New York: Teachers College Press.

Why Teachers Leave

25

Karianne Sparks and Leslie Keiler

Karianne Sparks is a graduate student at Villanova University, Pennsylvania. She can be reached by phone at (302) 478-5001 and by e-mail at earnersparks@yahoo.com. Leslie Keiler is Professor of Education at the University of Richmond, Virginia.

Every year too many teachers leave their classrooms for other careers, contributing to the teacher shortage in the United States. Newspapers across the country carry stories about schools calling retired teachers into service and states issuing increasing numbers of emergency certifications.

The stories of former teachers who left the classroom early in their careers may illuminate the problems that politicians and educators need to address in order to staunch the flow of teachers leaving U.S. classrooms. Six former teachers agreed to sit down with us to discuss their experiences and their decision to leave the profession. These former teachers represent a wide range of ages, teaching contexts, and personal characteristics. Three of them left the profession to go into higher education as computer educators:

- Abe,[1] age 31, who had taught special education at a small rural high school for three years.
- Imojen, 30, who had taught students with emotional disabilities and disorders at a large suburban elementary school for three years.
- Kayla, 30, who had taught English in middle schools and high schools in a large suburban community for four and one-half years.

---

[1] The names of all teachers mentioned in this chapter are pseudonyms.

The other three former teachers left to pursue a variety of alternative paths:

- Ethel, 24, had taught science at a small suburban middle school for two years. She is now a homemaker.
- Zoe, 21, had taught English for one year at a medium-sized suburban high school. She left to pursue graduate studies.
- George, 52, had taught elementary, middle, and high school social studies for eight years. He left to work in banking.

Overall Impressions of Teaching

Surprisingly, these six former teachers expressed positive overall feelings about teaching. They commented on the joy of working with students and helping them grow and learn every day. They also talked about their feelings of accomplishment as teachers. Their comments included "I felt I made a positive impact" (Abe), "Teaching was extremely rewarding" (George), and "The kids were wonderful" (Kayla). Interactions with their students, both formal and informal, made these people stay in teaching as long as they did. All of the interviewees had at least some positive things to say about the profession; in fact, many hesitated at first to discuss the negative aspects of the job.

However, the former teachers' responses began to shed light on the harsh realities of teaching when we asked them to provide details of negative experiences. Typical comments focused on pay and respect: "There are a lot of negatives to teaching. You don't get paid much. You get zero respect" (Kayla). Paperwork also garnered some complaints. As Abe said, "If you really want to find out whether someone wants to be a teacher, throw 100 pages of meaningless crap at them that they have to fill out each day, and if after a couple of weeks they still say, 'Bring it on!' then say, 'OK, you can be a teacher.'"

The negative descriptions, however, were eclipsed by the overwhelmingly positive comments that the interviewees made about being educators. Most of them clearly still believed in and admired the teaching profession. This positive attitude makes their defection from education even more unfortunate.

Varied Experiences with Administrators

The former teachers offered highly polarized comments about their experiences with administrators. Some of the positive descriptions included "They were very supportive and protective" (Kayla), and "My first administrator hired me, and he just loved me" (Imojen). Other former teachers recounted a lack of contact: "I hardly ever saw the principal" (Zoe). Still others experienced open hostility. For example, Abe's principal, angered that Abe had been hired to teach special education before he had completed his special education certification, told him, "The fact that you are here in this profession at all is an insult to me, an insult to this county, and an insult to this profession."

The former teachers' relationships with administrators did not seem to be the major cause of their decision to leave the profession; none of them directly blamed their administration for the change. But these relationships did influence the former teachers' overall feelings about the profession. Those who had suffered through horrible experiences with administrators were decidedly less enthusiastic about teaching in general than those who had enjoyed supportive administrators.

Mixed Collegial Support

With a few minor exceptions, the former teachers spoke warmly about their experiences with other teachers. George remarked, "I can't think of a negative experience I had with a colleague."

Others went further in describing the tremendous amount of support that they received from other teachers. Kayla talked about the beginning of her first year, when other teachers gave her a head start by making all her bulletin boards for her. Several teachers praised the wonderful advice that they had received from their mentors.

Unfortunately, at least one former teacher did not experience warmth and support. When asked about the other teachers in her department, Ethel commented, "I haven't really gotten a lot of support from them." Ethel also explained that her mentor taught at another school across town, a situation that made it hard for the two of them to meet. Other former teachers expressed dismay that meetings that could have facilitated discussion and support, such as department meetings, did not occur on a regular basis. In one case, collegial support consisted of the advice, "Get out while you still can!"

Low Salary, Lack of Respect

A few of the former teachers talked about the difficulty and accompanying stress of living on a teacher's salary. Abe, commenting on his decision to leave the profession, remarked, "A big part of that, quite frankly, is the pay."

Most of the former teachers, however, denied that salary had directly influenced their decision to leave the profession. At the same time, they made many references to low teacher pay that contradicted these claims. They explained that although salary itself was not important, what it represented did matter to them. As Imojen said, "It's not the salary. If people respect the work that you do, then it's OK. But some people don't respect the work that you do because they think they can do it better."

To these teachers, the low pay reflected a lack of community respect that contributed to their decision to leave teaching. The subsequent career choices they made support the impression that salary affected their decision. At least four of the six interviewees currently make significantly more money than they did as teachers, even though they remain in related fields. Thus, although most of the former teachers may not have made conscious decisions on the basis of salary, their low pay clearly contributed to their actions.

High Stress Levels

All the former teachers discussed the high levels of stress that teachers endure every day. Some of the stress stemmed from such mundane sources as paperwork; some came from more serious sources, such as parental criticism or student violence. The former teachers said that they were emotionally and physically drained at the end of each school year. Several of them spoke about parental hostility and lack of support, citing experiences with parents who thought that they knew the profession better than the teachers. Teachers who believed that parents or others in the community did not respect them had a more negative view of the profession as a whole.

An additional factor that contributed to the teachers' stress was the enormous commitment they felt toward their students' well-being. As Ethel said, "A lot of times you spend more time being the parent than you do teaching students the content knowledge that you love so much. You have to try to overcome that barrier. Some of the kids haven't even eaten breakfast, and I'm trying to teach them about science."

George described how he became known as the teacher who could "handle" the tougher students; he related to those students in a way that many other teachers did not. But according to George, his administrators did not realize that giving all the troubled students to him would present a problem, and for years he taught the toughest classes. He explained, "I left the profession because it mentally and emotionally drained me."

Other teachers experienced the threat of physical violence from their students. Two of the six interviewees reported that a student had brought a gun into their classrooms. Although neither of the students used the gun, the possibility of violence generated enormous stress for these teachers at the time and in subsequent interactions with students. Another former teacher discussed incidents in which colleagues had been bitten, hit, or otherwise injured by students.

The Decision to Leave Teaching

When asked to describe their decision to leave teaching, several teachers cited feelings of exhaustion or lethargy. One had sought help from a therapist. Another cited her desire to have some time off from the "grind" of teaching to write and do research. Others discussed the fact that their lives as teachers lacked creativity, challenge, and intellectual stimulation. As Kayla said:

> I really believe that there is some science in teaching, but I believe it's also an art, a creative process. . . . The school district officials said that teachers had to teach the same content, on the same day, in the same way, so that they could be sure that every student was getting the same instruction to prepare them for the state assessments. That's a very interesting idea, and I'm not sure it's totally terrible. But it doesn't account for the differences in the students, and it makes teaching a very boring career choice at this point.

This teacher could not bear the prospect of continuing to teach without the creative outlets that she perceived to be diminishing in the profession.

The former teachers did not take their decision to leave lightly. Several of them expressed uncertainty about their future and a desire to return to teaching some day. When asked whether or not he believed he would return to the profession, Abe mused about a future scenario in which he earned enough money to not have to worry about himself and his family. He indicated that such a situation would definitely encourage him to go back to teaching. George also spoke longingly of the day when he would be a teacher again. When asked whether he would return to the profession, he responded, "I hope so, I hope so!" Nearly all of the teachers communicated the belief that they had not truly left the profession, but had simply taken some time off from the everyday stress of teaching. Although none of the former teachers had immediate plans to return to the classroom, none ruled it out for the future.

How Can Schools Keep Good Teachers?

The former teachers spoke of teaching as an honorable profession. The ability to affect the lives of young people provided them with a sense of accomplishment that many professionals never experience. Yet these six teachers chose to leave the profession after relatively short careers. Why?

The answer is both complicated and simple. For these former teachers, it was not one specific incident that drove them from the classroom, but rather a series of disappointments and frustrations. Overwhelming paperwork, low salary, and many other factors contributed to their decision to leave. All the people with whom the teachers came into contact on a regular basis affected their feelings about teaching. Contact with students resulted in positive effects, whereas negative effects came from unsupportive administrators, uninvolved parents, legislators who dictated the curriculum, and community members who failed to appreciate teachers.

The stories of these six former teachers suggest ways to keep good teachers in our classrooms. Salaries that not only make it possible for teachers to support their families, but also enable them to hold their heads high in their communities, are crucial for the long-term health of public education. None of the teachers mentioned colleagues as the main reason that they left the profession, but some of the younger teachers suggested that they might have lengthened their stay if they could have relied on the regular and consistent support of other staff members. More active support from administrators is also essential; early-career teachers need support and protection in their interactions with critical parents, potentially violent students, and communities that undervalue their contributions. By taking these steps and attending to the needs of early-career teachers, we can provide the consistent and significant support that will prevent more good teachers from leaving education.

26

The Qualities
of Great Teachers

Mark F. Goldberg

Mark F. Goldberg is an education writer and editor in Austin, Texas. He can be reached by phone at (512) 257-7971 and by e-mail at mark12738@aol.com.

Greatness in teaching is just as rare as greatness in medicine, dance, law, or any other profession. Although the qualities that make great teachers are not easy to inculcate or duplicate, understanding these qualities can give all teachers a standard of excellence to strive for, and guide schools in their efforts to recruit and retain the best teachers.

To that end, I offer the following observations about the key characteristics of great teachers. This list is certainly not exhaustive, and the characteristics do not appear in any particular order of importance. In my more than 40 years in education, including 24 years as a public school administrator who directly supervised more than 130 different teachers, these qualities emerged as hallmarks of the best teaching.

Willingness to Put in the Necessary Time

You cannot achieve greatness by working from 8:30 a.m. to 3:00 p.m. Teaching, like every other serious profession, requires time. Dennis Littky, an award-winning principal, said, "You can't be a great teacher or principal and not work long, long hours" (personal communication, November 11, 1988). By investing time—to prepare for class, to go over student work, to meet students outside of class, to talk to parents, to attend school meetings, and to serve on school committees—a great teacher indicates to students that she or he sincerely cares about their learning.

When well-known and respected teacher Thomas T. Lyons retired from Phillips Academy in Andover, Massachusetts, after a 36-year career, the many tributes he received from former students overwhelmingly focused on the time he spent with them (Rimer, 1999). Lyons interviewed every youngster individually at the beginning of the school year. One student, Julie Stephens, said, "Mr. Lyons must have invested at least 20 hours in me" just on one paper (p. A6).

Most teachers belong to a teachers' association, union, or other organization that represents their interests. Typically, some formal document or agreement specifies how many minutes per day or hours per week they must teach; how much unstructured time they are entitled to; how many meetings they must attend; and the compensation they must receive for additional work beyond the usual load. Great teachers respect this agreement and acknowledge that it protects their rights, ensures academic freedom, and spells out good professional working conditions. But they don't hesitate to go beyond the contract voluntarily and often—for example, by meeting with a student study group during the teacher's preparation period or after school—in order to meet the needs of their students.

Love for the Age Group They Teach

My wife, who had a successful 32-year career in elementary education, had a natural affinity for the early primary grades and grew increasingly uncomfortable with each grade above the 2nd. She read children's literature for younger students with gusto, happily attended workshops to master materials and methods to better teach primary math and science, and loved spending time with young children. But teaching above grade 4, she was a fish out of water.

About 25 years ago, when the shift from junior high schools to middle schools took hold, I came across many teachers who wanted to work with children of middle school age, 11 to 14, and who took pleasure in the special challenges that those years posed. In many districts, the frequent requests to transfer from junior to senior high school slowed or nearly stopped. Many middle schools developed advisory groups and used a team approach to bring teachers and students into closer contact. Teachers who had previously felt uncomfortable in junior high schools thrived in the middle grades, and a cadre of great middle school teachers emerged.

Most teachers find joy in teaching because of their talent for relating to students in a particular age group. Unfortunately, too many school districts transfer teachers on the basis of seniority from one grade to another without recognizing the importance of fit. An important part of greatness is the match between the teacher's skills and interests and the age of his or her students. A great middle school English teacher might be an average 11th or 12th grade English teacher.

An Effective Classroom Management Style

Great teachers need to find their own ways to "manage" a group of students. For instance, if a student were to interrupt the class inappropriately, Lee Canter's Assertive Discipline approach (Canter & Canter, 2002) would suggest consequences for failure to follow known and reasonable rules; Alfie Kohn (1996) might suggest that the teacher ask himself or herself whether the content or methods of the lesson contributed to the problem. The most effective teachers draw from these well-known theories, but adapt them to their own personality.

Because great teachers develop and hone their own classroom management style, their techniques vary. All, however, have at least the following common characteristics in their classrooms:

- Few behavior problems.
- A culture of respect that flows in every direction: teacher to students, students to teacher, students to students, and everyone to guests.
- Immediate—or at least timely—teacher actions that usually work.
- A clear, shared understanding of acceptable and appropriate behavior.

Positive Relationships with Other Adults

Too often, we underestimate the amount of time that teachers spend with other adults in a school—other teachers, administrators, and parents. Great teachers work well with each of these groups.

They depend on other teachers as a constant source of information, enrichment, and sometimes solace. From study groups to faculty meetings to such rare moments as receiving an award or attending the funeral of a student, teachers need to support one another. Outstanding teachers quickly become identified as school leaders, whom other teachers admire and turn to for advice or collegial sharing.

The best teachers also find ways to work harmoniously with administrators and to show administrators how they can support teachers. For example, the teacher may point out areas of the curriculum that need attention and coordinate or offer to serve on a committee to explore solutions to a problem.

Great teachers also place a priority on keeping parents informed about their children's progress, and they sensitively help parents understand their children's problems. These teachers understand that the lack of a strong partnership between teachers and families may undo many of their best efforts.

Consistent Excellence

Greatness in teaching requires consistently outstanding performance over the years. That does not mean that the teacher never has a bad day, or even a bad week. In fact, most great teachers have had a difficult year or two. One of the finest English teachers I knew had a tough year adjusting to a new school, and a somewhat spotty year about seven years later when serious family problems were weighing heavily on him. Over the 19 years that I supervised him, however, he had 17 great years and two good years during which he showed remarkable resilience and fortitude.

The best teachers get divorced, become ill, have problems with their own children, need to attend to aging parents, and have other personal issues in the same proportion as other professionals. They also have both mild and serious professional disagreements about new curriculums, teaching methods, assessment techniques, and materials. But great teachers have the good judgment required to balance these problems in a way that minimizes fluctuations in classroom performance.

Some teachers are able to compartmentalize personal and other issues; others require a short period of time off to handle vexing problems. The best teachers consistently find ways to integrate new methods in an ever-changing profession into their successful practices. Dedication to their work, flexibility, and the willingness to grow are common to great teachers in the face of difficulty and change.

Expert Use of Instructional Methods

Great teachers use a variety of instructional methods that they feel comfortable with; within the same school, you'll find different teachers getting excellent results using such methods as mini-lectures and interactive lectures, problem-based learning, cooperative groups, and multiple intelligences approaches. No single teaching method or approach works best for every teacher with every student.

We know, however, that research and experience strongly support some instructional approaches over others. The best teachers select from the methods that are well researched and widely practiced at their grade level or within their subject area, and become expert in several that fit their style and the needs of their students at that time.

In-Depth Content Knowledge

Both progressive and conservative educators speak about the importance of content. From Deborah Meier, the MacArthur award-winning advocate of small schools of choice, to William Bennett, the former education secretary and critic of public schools, educators emphasize the importance of knowing the subject you teach. Everyone agrees that great teachers possess a solid command of content, whether their expertise lies in knowledge of reading in the early elementary grades or a serious command of biology or mathematics at the high school level.

Because of the close connection between preparation time and content, the best teachers often spend as much time preparing for a class as they do teaching it. Setting up a lab experiment for 5th graders, reading a short story three times in order to formulate good questions for discussion, or working through 15 math problems and anticipating questions and obstacles takes time and deepens the great teacher's mastery of content.

Capacity for Growth

Like any other profession, teaching undergoes constant change. The past 30 years have witnessed a marked increase in education research and the emergence of solid information about teaching and learning. Great teachers remain intellectually alive and open to responsible change grounded in theory, research, and practice. Dozens of specific and well-researched techniques are available today to help all learners—particularly reluctant learners and those with disabilities. Since the late 1970s, all of the following areas of education knowledge (and many others) have developed and become worth exploring: technology; character education; rubrics; closing the achievement gap; standards; cooperative learning; diversity; assessment and evaluation; multiple intelligences; reading instruction; curriculum reform; and bilingual education/structured English immersion.

The much-used phrase "lifelong learner" really does apply. Although any great teacher must judiciously decide what is worth pursuing and how to maintain high standards, only a Luddite would ignore the potential of new methods for using technology, research on the most effective strategies for reading instruction, or current cooperative learning approaches.

Of course, content knowledge is an important area of growth. Great teachers are always learning more about math for elementary students, science for disabled students, or Shakespeare for Advanced Placement students. In addition, outstanding teachers continually grow by taking college and inservice courses, reading professional literature, and engaging others in serious conversation about school issues. Often, the finest teachers serve on education committees or become teacher experts who lead study groups or professional development courses.

Steadiness of Purpose and Teaching Personality

Some people, particularly people outside the profession, expect teachers to "perform" in classrooms and to maintain a high energy level. Great teachers, however, are not necessarily performers. Instead, they hold students' attention through subject mastery, skillful lesson design, actions that demonstrate caring, and an honesty that reveals their individual personality.

After all, K–12 teachers conduct formal teaching for about 25 hours each week, 40 weeks each year—plus individual conferences, hall duty, informal meetings, and other contacts with students. No one can sustain a performance for that length of time. The great teacher is steady, intelligent, concerned, interesting, and interested. The performers do not last long.

A Complex Act

No one can produce a complete and definitive list of the characteristics of great classroom teaching, but I hope that this list provides a starting place. Knowing the qualities of greatness can help teachers strive for the highest standards and help education professors, teachers, and administrators jointly craft preservice training or inservice programs that build on these qualities.

Teaching is a complex act. Danielson (1996) estimates that a teacher makes more than 3,000 nontrivial decisions every day. No list can capture the extraordinary subtlety involved in making instant decisions about which student to call on, how to frame an impromptu question, or how to respond to an interruption. The late Madeline Hunter compared teaching to surgery, "where you think fast on your feet and do the best you can with the information you have. You must be very skilled, very knowledgeable, and exquisitely well trained, because neither the teacher nor the surgeon can say, 'Everybody sit still until I figure out what in the heck we're gonna do next'" (Goldberg, 1990, p. 43).

Watching a great teacher at the top of his or her form is like watching a great surgical or artistic performance. Although infinitely difficult and painstakingly planned, great teaching appears effortless and seamless. One can easily believe that it is the simplest thing in the world—until one tries to do it.

References

Canter, L., & Canter, M. (2002). *Assertive discipline: Positive behavior management for today's classroom* (3rd ed.). Los Angeles: Lee Canter & Associates.

Danielson, C. (1996). *Enhancing professional practice: A framework for teaching.* Alexandria, VA: Association for Supervision and Curriculum Development.

Goldberg, M. (1990). Portrait of Madeline Hunter. *Educational Leadership, 47*(5), 41–43.

Kohn, A. (1996). *Beyond discipline: From compliance to community.* Alexandria, VA: Association for Supervision and Curriculum Development.

Rimer, S. (1999, July 31). Teaching as a torrent of bubbling information. *New York Times,* p. A6.

Index

Page references for figures are followed by *f*, as in 35*f*.

About the Editor

Marge Scherer is Editor in Chief of ASCD's *Educational Leadership*. A former classroom teacher, she has received national awards for her writing on education topics. A recent interview, "Do Students Care About Learning? A Conversation with Mihaly Csikszentmihalyi" (*Educational Leadership*, 2002), was a finalist in the Distinguished Achievement Awards competition sponsored by the Association of Educational Publishers. You may reach Marge at el@ascd.org.